MONICA SELES

MONICA SELES

Rose Blue and Corinne J. Naden

Introduction by James Scott Brady,
Trustee, the Center to Prevent Handgun Violence
Vice Chairman, the Brain Injury Foundation

Chelsea House Publishers
Philadelphia

Frontispiece: Monica Seles flashes a smile after another victory. The superstar has fought through many catastrophes during her career, including a stabbing in 1993.

CHELSEA HOUSE PUBLISHERS

EDITOR IN CHIEF Sally Cheney
DIRECTOR OF PRODUCTION Kim Shinners
PRODUCTION MANAGER Pamela Loos
ART DIRECTOR Sara Davis
SENIOR EDITOR LeeAnne Gelletly
PRODUCTION EDITOR Diann Grasse
COVER DESIGNER Keith Trego
LAYOUT 21st Century Publishing and Communications, Inc.

First Printing

1 3 5 7 9 8 6 4 2

The Chelsea House World Wide Web address is
http://www.chelseahouse.com

CIP applied for ISBN 0-7910-5899-9 (HC)

CONTENTS

OVERCOMING ADVERSITY

ON FACING ADVERSITY

James Scott Brady

I GUESS IT'S a long way from a Centralia, Illinois, train yard to the George Washington University Hospital Trauma Unit. My dad was a yardmaster for the old Chicago, Burlington & Quincy Railroad. As a child, I used to get to sit in the engineer's lap and imagine what it was like to drive that train. I guess I always have liked being in the "driver's seat."

Years later, however, my interest turned from driving trains to driving campaigns. In 1979, former Texas governor John Connally hired me as a press secretary in his campaign for the American presidency. We lost the Republican primary to a former Hollywood star named Ronald Reagan. But I managed to jump over to the Reagan campaign. When Reagan was elected in 1980, I was "sitting in the catbird seat," as humorist James Thurber would say—poised to be named presidential press secretary. I held that title throughout the eight years of the Reagan administration. But not without one terrible, extended interruption.

It happened barely two months after the Reagan administration took office. I never even heard the shots. On March 30, 1981, my life went blank in an instant. In an attempt to assassinate President Reagan, John Hinckley Jr. armed himself with a "Saturday night special"—a low-quality, $29 pistol—and shot wildly as our presidential entourage exited a Washington hotel. One of the exploding bullets struck me just above the left eye. It shattered into a couple dozen fragments, some of which penetrated my skull and entered my brain.

The next few months of my life were a nightmare of repeated surgery, broken contact with the outside world, and a variety of medical complications. More than once, I was very close to death.

The next few years were filled with frustrating struggles to function with a paralyzed right side, struggles to speak and communicate.

To people who face and defeat daunting obstacles, "ambition" is not becoming wealthy or famous or winning elections or awards. Words like "ambition" and "achievement" and "success" take on very different meanings. The objective is just to live, to wake up every morning. The goals are not lofty; they are very ordinary.

My own heroes are ordinary folks—but they accomplish extraordinary things because they try. My greatest hero is my wife, Sarah. She's accomplished a lot of things in life, but two stand out. The first has been the way she has cared for me and our son since I was shot. A tremendous tragedy and burden was dropped unexpectedly into her life, totally beyond her control and without justification. She could have given up; instead, she focused her energies on preserving our family and returning our lives to normal as much as possible. Week by week, month by month, year by year, she has not reached for the miraculous, just for the normal. Yet in focusing on the normal, she has helped accomplish the miraculous.

Her other most remarkable accomplishment, to me, has been spearheading the effort to keep guns out of the hands of criminals and children in America. Opponents call her a "gun grabber"; I call her a national hero. And I am not alone.

After a seven-year battle, during which Sarah and I worked tirelessly to educate the public about the need for stronger gun laws, the Brady Bill became law in 1993. It was a victory, achieved in the face of tremendous opposition, that now benefits all Americans. From the time the law took effect through fall 1997, background checks had stopped 173,000 criminals and other high-risk purchasers from buying handguns, and the law has helped to reduce illegal gun trafficking.

Sarah was not pursuing fame, or even recognition. She simply started at one point—when our son, Scott, found a loaded handgun on the seat of a pickup truck and, thinking it was a toy, pointed it at Sarah.

Fortunately, no one was hurt. But seeing a gun nearly bring a second tragedy upon our family, Sarah became determined to do whatever she could to prevent senseless death and injury from guns.

Some people think of Sarah as a powerful political force. To me, she's the person who so many times fed me and helped me dress during my long years of recovery.

Overcoming obstacles is part of life, not just for people who are challenged by disabilities, illnesses, or tragedies, but for all people. No matter what the obstacle—fear, disability, prejudice, grief, or a difficulty that isn't likely to "just go away"—we can all work to make this world a better place.

With her parents cheering behind her, Monica celebrates her return to tennis at an exhibition match against veteran Martina Navratilova in 1995.

1

THE COMEBACK

GRASPING HER RACKET firmly in hand, the tall 21-year-old woman, her long brown hair scooped back in a neat ponytail, strode nervously onto the center of the tennis court of the Atlantic City arena amidst a noisy uproar. Her blue-green eyes swept over the faces of thousands of joyous fans, who stood as they stomped, clapped, and cheered wildly in ovation. It was an overwhelming reception for the smiling tennis pro, who at first covered her face with her hands, then bowed and curtseyed to the ever-appreciative crowd. They in turn applauded even louder, thrilled to see that their favorite star, Monica Seles, had finally returned to the tennis courts.

Monica had achieved the top ranking of her career very early in life. In 1991, at the age of 19, Seles had knocked the top-ranked Steffi Graf from the number one position, and had maintained that top position for almost two years. It is likely she would have remained number one for much longer, but in the spring of 1993, at the height of her career, Monica Seles became a victim of violence. While on her home turf—

the tennis court—and in the midst of a match, she had been attacked by a knife-wielding assailant.

The resulting physical injury had taken a few weeks to recover from; but the emotional damage had been far greater. Monica was left so devastated by the attack that she feared she would never again set foot on any tennis court, much less a professional one. She had undergone an agonizing search to make sense of what happened to her and to learn how to cope. That journey had taken more than two years—and during that entire time she had removed herself from the women's tennis circuit. On July 29, 1995, after a 26-month absence from women's tennis, Monica Seles felt ready to make her mark once more.

Monica was making her tennis comeback at an exhibition match with superstar and friend 38-year-old Martina Navratilova, who had herself recently retired from professional tennis. A *match* refers to a tennis contest, which in men's professional competition is won by taking three out of five sets, and in women's tennis two out of three sets. To win a *set,* the player must win six *games* (each game is won by taking four points: scored as 15, 30, 40, game—but must be won by two points).

Exhibition matches are played for money but do not count on a player's record. Navratilova thought it an ideal way to ease Seles back into competition.

The media had responded to the news of the Seles-Navratilova match with enthusiasm. CBS Sports president David Kenin included the following statement in a June 6, 1995, press release about the event:

> We are ecstatic that CBS Sports will showcase Monica Seles' return to competitive tennis. Her absence during the past twenty-six months has left the sports world without one of its brightest stars. The match, which features two illustrious champions, already registers as a victory for Seles—signifying a triumph of spirit in overcoming a harrowing incident.

The match became a bit of a glitzy show business production as well, taking place at the New Jersey shore's gambling paradise in Atlantic City. The day before the match, Seles flew by private jet to New Jersey from Florida, then took a stretch limousine to Caesar's Palace on the Boardwalk. There she found a red carpet leading the way from her car to the hotel entrance and a welcoming throng, including a costumed Caesar and Cleopatra, and young girls tossing rose petals at her feet. She told the crowd of fans, reporters, and photographers who greeted her, "I'm just going to play great tennis and have fun."

Still, the next day proved stressful. Monica later described how she entered the Atlantic City arena feeling very nervous and hearing her heart pounding in her ears. But she later admitted that although the event over-whelmed her, she felt a welcome sense of relief as well: "The spectators were on their feet, and their cries of support drowned out the beat of my heart. . . . I'm home, I thought as I walked out, I'm home."

As she prepared to begin the match, a determined Seles turned to face Navratilova. She may have been back at home on the court, but she was still nervous. The umpire called, "Seles to serve," and the game was on. Seles promptly double faulted—placed both served balls outside the court—and thus gave the point to Navratilova.

"I was so nervous during the first game," she recalled later, "that when I threw the ball up to serve, I couldn't see it. My legs were numb." But she persevered and soon won the first set, 6–3. After she broke Martina's serve in the second set, she felt back in the swing of things. Although her nerves kept betraying her and she kept double faulting, she did win the match by taking the second set, 6–2.

At the end of the set, Seles ran to the net to hug her opponent. Said Navratilova as they left the court, "You're back, girl. There's no question in my mind, you're back." Monica Seles couldn't stop smiling. She

Monica waves to fans after winning a first-round game of the 1996 French Open. In the early 1990s, she had taken the French Open title for three consecutive years.

was definitely back on track, ready and able to show others—as well as herself—what she was capable of. It had taken her a long time to step back on the tennis court, but she had done it.

Although many professional athletes share Monica's drive and natural ability, few have had to deal with the trauma that she faced. But with the love and support of her family, the help of professionals and friends, and through her own perseverance, Monica has made it. She exemplifies a true athlete, one who despite adversity and hardship, can come back and perform at the highest level. After a long struggle, she found a way to return to the way of life she had known and the sport she had loved since she was six years old.

A young Monica delivers her patented two-hand forehand shot. During her childhood in the former Yugoslavia, Monica began playing tennis at the early age of six.

2

RISING STAR

THE YOUNG GIRL who would one day rule the tennis world was born on December 2, 1973, in the European city of Novi Sad, located on the Danube River in northern Yugoslavia. The country had been formed in 1929 from the kingdoms of Serbs, Croats, and Slovenes, along with the independent state of Montenegro.

It was not an easy alliance. Since World War II, Yugoslavia had been kept together by the stern hand of Communist leader Josip Broz, known to the world as Marshal Tito. Monica's family knew what it meant to live under harsh rule. Her grandfather was sent to a prison camp because his beliefs differed from the government's. Her grandmother was a devout Catholic who took her faith seriously in a country where religion was illegal.

At the time of Monica's birth, her country was sailing an often bumpy but generally steady course through the second half of the 20th century. However, hard times were not far ahead. In 1991 Yugoslavia would break up into the countries of Serbia and

Montenegro, and Serbia would lay claim to the city of Novi Sad, Monica's birthplace.

Monica's parents were educated and very attentive to their children. Karolj Seles made documentary films and had been a physical education major in college. Esther Seles was a computer programmer. Their first child, Zoltan, was eight years older than Monica.

As a teenager, Zoltan became a great fan of Swedish tennis great Bjorn Borg. When the young boy told his father that he would like to learn tennis, Karolj Seles responded with enthusiasm. Unfortunately, he had no idea how to play the game and there were no instructors in Novi Sad. Although there were four tennis courts available, there wasn't a shop to buy a tennis racket. Karolj solved the problem by driving over into Italy—a 10-hour trip—to buy one. He solved the need for an instructor by browsing through bookstores in Novi Sad until he found an old paperback on playing the game. Soon afterward Zoltan began his training in tennis.

One of the most significant events in Monica's life occurred at the age of six, when she decided that she too wanted to play tennis, just like her older brother, Zoltan. When Monica announced her interest, her father simply nodded and headed back to Italy for another racket.

Monica loved her little wooden tennis racket, which she carried everywhere and kept close by while she slept. But when she played tennis, she did not hold it correctly, at least according to the instruction book. Normally, a tennis player holds the racket in one hand, right or left. But whether hitting forehand or backhand, Monica's natural inclination was to hold the racket in both hands. Her brother tried to tell her that her grip was wrong, but her father said she should do what felt natural to her. As it turned out, her father gave young Monica good advice. This two-fisted approach for hitting may have been unusual, but it allowed Seles to smack the ball with great force. That, coupled with her own natural athletic strength, made her a fearsome opponent on the court.

Soon Monica couldn't get enough of tennis. She and Zoltan would practice by bouncing the ball off the brick wall of their apartment building. Unfortunately tennis courts were rarely available for play in Novi Sad. So Monica, her brother, and father would string a net across the parking lot of their apartment building and play there.

The young girl loved playing the game, and her father was a very patient teacher. He tried not to push his children but to encourage them. Sometimes, he used his talents as an artist to teach them, drawing cartoon characters to illustrate differences in various tennis techniques or to demonstrate how to perform proper strokes and serves. At other times, he tried to motivate Monica, using the cartoon characters Tom and Jerry. Karolj drew Jerry, the mouse, on the tennis balls and encouraged Monica to pretend she was Tom, the cat, chasing after Jerry.

While Monica and Zoltan were developing their game under the patient eye of their father, their mother was not so pleased. She thought her daughter should be playing with her dolls, not slamming a ball around the parking lot night and day. And Monica's grandmother agreed. "It's not normal for a little girl," she complained. But it was normal for this young girl. She tried to explain to her grandmother that she simply loved to play the game. Eventually, Monica's mother came around, realizing that playing tennis certainly seemed to make her daughter happy. As she admitted to Monica's grandmother, "It is her personality to play."

Karolj Seles must have been a good tennis coach: within a year of his teaching, Zoltan was a top ranked junior player in Europe. Monica entered her first tournament when she was six and a half years old and came in third. It was beginning to look like all those hours in the parking lot were paying off.

Monica and her family lived in an apartment building similar to this one in Novi Sad, a city in the former Yugoslavia. With no tennis court to play on, Monica, her father, and her brother, Zoltan, improvised by stringing a net across the parking lot of their complex.

Of course, life was not all tennis, even in the Seles household. Monica went to school like any other child in Yugoslavia. She studied and she acted in school plays. As a young girl, she created costumes for her Barbie dolls and teddy bears, and begged her mother for help in creating new outfits for herself. Monica was fascinated by the world of fashion. The woman who ran the corner newsstand near their apartment building let her borrow fashion magazines such as *Vogue, Elle,* and

Cosmopolitan, and she pored over pictures of dresses by designers like Armani, Versace, and Chanel.

The years passed and the kid training to play tennis in a parking lot became stronger and more versatile on the court. She led an exciting life, participating in tournaments in various countries. By the time she was eight years old, she was the number one junior player in Yugoslavia. At age 10, she was the European 12-and-under champ. At age 11, in 1985, she was the Yugoslavian Sportswoman of the Year.

Although it looked like Monica's tennis career was really taking off, she was actually at a disadvantage compared with most young players. Because tennis was not a big sport in Novi Sad, there were few opportunities in her hometown to practice. None of the four tennis courts in the town was indoors, making practice time more precious, especially during Yugoslavia's freezing winters. When it was cold, Monica had to practice on indoor volleyball courts or on walls of the local gymnasium. In addition, all the Novi Sad tennis courts had clay surfaces. She did not have the opportunity to practice on other kinds of court surfaces, such as composition asphalt and grass. Because tennis balls bounce differently on each of these surfaces, serious tennis players should practice on all kinds of courts.

Not having the advantage of testing different kinds of tennis courts should have been a drawback for Monica. However, it did not seem to affect her performance; in her early years she won tournament after tournament. Yet she and her father knew that, despite her extraordinary talent, her tennis career could go only so far under these conditions.

Players wanting to get to the top in the world of professional tennis have to play the tournaments, wherever and whenever they are held. Standings in those tournaments help to determine seeding, or placement, in upcoming tournaments. Monica understood that the better her seeding in tournaments, the better her chances of playing the best opponents and improving. So, she and her father traveled to as many tournaments as time and money would permit. A visa out of Yugoslavia was not easy to get at that time. But, like other sports stars all over the world, Monica found that her government would grant her the privilege to travel outside the country because of her success. So, on occasion, she and her father visited the United States.

In 1985 Monica Seles and her father went to Miami, Florida, where she caught the eye of coach Nick Bollettieri. He offered 12-year-old Monica the chance to train at his famed tennis academy in Bradenton, Florida, along with her family. Although she was hesitant at first about accepting, her father urged her to accept the offer of two free weeks of sunshine and expert coaching. Monica was instantly enchanted with everything in Bradenton—the warm weather, the different types of courts, and the intense, dedicated instruction. But the death of her grandmother cut short her time at the academy and hastened the family's return to Yugoslavia.

Monica returned to her homeland for one more year. Within a few years, Yugoslavia would undergo major changes, and Monica could never go back to what she had known before. Yugoslavia's longtime leader, Marshal Tito, had died in 1980 and the country was being run by a collective Communist presidency. In 1990, after the Communist party renounced its leadership of the country, the states of Croatia and Slovenia would declare independence, and fighting would ensue between the Croats and the ethnic Serbs who lived there.

The bordering Serbia, where Seles was born, would send in arms and medical supplies and clash with the Yugoslav army. Soon afterward Serbia and Montenegro would declare themselves the Federal Republic of Yugoslavia, while Serbia would send arms into nearby

Monica fortunately had much support from her mother, Esther, and her father, Karolj, who was also Monica's coach during her junior tennis career.

Bosnia and Herzegovina, the remaining states of the former Yugoslavia. For the next several years, a terrible wave of slaughter of ethnic peoples, including Serbs and Albanians, would tear apart Monica's country.

Because Monica Seles and her family had left the country, however, they were spared from the trauma of the conflict. In 1986, the Seles family had once more flown to Florida, this time for the Orange Bowl tournament. By this time she was, at 13 years old, the world's number one junior tennis player.

A little boy prays near the grave of his father, killed by a mortar bomb, in the Bosnian capital of Sarajevo. Monica and her family lived not far from the war zone in eastern Europe, and were fortunate to move to the United States before fighting got out of control.

Bollettieri was also at the Orange Bowl, and he had not forgotten Monica. This time, he told her parents that he was offering Monica a full scholarship to his tennis academy. Zoltan was invited, too. Thrilled with the idea of what the academy could do for her tennis game, Monica planned to move to Florida.

Monica and Zoltan came to the United States without their parents, who could not quit their jobs to accompany their children. Although the brother and sister tennis students had each other, they had difficulty adjusting to life in America. Monica was 13 years old and away from her parents for the first time. Although both she and Zoltan had learned some English at school in Yugoslavia, neither was comfortable yet with the language.

Monica's main reason for being in Florida was, of course, to concentrate on her tennis game, which she did. And she learned from the best. Nicholas James Bollettieri has a love of the game and a knack for turning out the great players. Born in Pelham, New York, in 1931, he became a teaching tennis pro in 1958 and went on to open the Bollettieri Academy, which has become a virtual assembly line for champions. Among his more famous tennis graduates are Andre Agassi, Jim Courier, Mary Pierce, and, of course, Monica Seles.

However, even the Nick Bollettieri Tennis Academy in Bradenton is not all tennis. One of the criticisms of the professional tour, especially in this era of multimedia coverage and soaring tournament prize money, is that there has been a rush to build the power game of budding tennis stars. As a result, their educational and social well-being has sometimes been sacrificed, as the tennis world would observe with one of Monica's peers—Jennifer Capriati—a tennis prodigy who would quickly rise and fall during the 1990s. Partly due to mounting criticism and partly to Capriati's troubles, in 1994 officials would impose a limit preventing players under the age of 14 years old from joining the professional circuit. Critics argued that even that age is still too low.

Monica and Zoltan moved into an academy-owned apartment. At first, the excitement of a new place and new tennis coaches was more than enough to keep Monica from missing her parents too badly. And when she wasn't practicing tennis, she was in school. Monica tried hard to adjust during those first few weeks, but her grades in some classes were low. Her biggest problem was that she couldn't understand English very well. In Monica's auto-biography, *Monica: From Fear to Victory*, she recalled her difficulties: "I was struggling with English, so how could I understand [Literature and American History]? Back home we learned the British way to speak and write, which is very proper. But in the U.S. there was so much slang, so many different accents."

However, Monica was good in mathematics, which has a universal language. And Zoltan, who spoke better English than his sister, tried his best to help her with her other classes.

Monica felt bad enough about her slipping grades, but she felt even worse about her slipping tennis game. The coaches at the academy had decided to change her two-fisted forehand into a one-handed stroke. The result was that for the first time in her young tennis life, Monica began to lose matches consistently.

Despondent over her problems with school and tennis, after five months she did what she had promised herself she would not do. She told her parents, who called her and her brother each week, that if they could not come to the United States, she would have to go home. Although only 13 years old, Monica was fully aware that her parents could not just easily leave their jobs and their lives behind to come to the United States. But she had to let them know how she felt. They told her they would think the decision over.

About a week later, Karolj and Esther Seles had a solution. They would take a leave of absence from their jobs and come to the United States for six months. With a little luck, they believed, Monica's father might be able to do some freelance cartoon work to earn money. Shortly after their arrival in Bradenton, Monica's family moved into an apartment provided by the academy.

Once he saw Monica practicing at the academy, how-ever, Karolj Seles was furious. The coaches had changed her two-fisted grip! He was certain that her own natural way of playing was the way she should play. Soon Monica went back to using her two-fisted forehand and backhand, and her father went back to being her coach.

As Monica improved her game, Zoltan started to lose interest in the sport. Monica has said that her brother has far more natural talent than she, but not the fire for the game that she has always possessed. It is the passion that compels her to be better, and the lack of it that let Zoltan Seles walk away from the professional courts. He left the academy after several months.

Although they had tried to change Monica's technique, the coaches at the tennis academy had been impressed with the strength of her strokes. Because she was more aggressive and stronger than most of the young girls on the courts, they began to arrange for her to play against the boys at the academy. Two of her opponents would become tennis champions—Andre Agassi and Jim Courier.

With her parents in the United States and her father as coach, a happier Monica Seles began to improve in her class work and on the tennis court. She didn't play in any junior tournaments during this period at the request of not her coaches but her parents. Her father believed that the less the players in the professional ranks knew about the unusual, hard-hitting style of his daughter, the greater her initial impact on the world of professional tennis.

Just what is this life of professional tennis that Monica and her family strove for? The distinction between amateur and professional player is often based on one thing—money. Amateur tennis players do not get prize money, although if they win a tournament they may get expenses paid for hotels, food, and travel. Amateur status makes players eligible for a tennis scholarship at a college or university. Once they turn pro, that eligibility is lost. However, pros are able to earn prize money, which during the past few decades has become very big indeed. Superstar players can earn several million dollars in the course of his or her career.

But it's not an easy life. It costs a great deal of money to compete as a professional tennis player, as Monica explained in her autobiography: "There are a lot of expenses—travel, hitting partners, physical therapists, coaches, hotels. Unlike team sports, expenses [for professional tennis] are sizable and are left to the individual."

And the schedule of a professional tennis player can be brutal, with tournaments taking place throughout the year. For all intents, the pro tour opens in January with the Australian Open tournament and ends with the U.S. Open in September. It's a world of practice, play, travel to the next tournament, practice, play, travel to the next tournament, and so on. It's not for the weak or faint hearted. Even most of the strong hearted don't make it to the top.

The top can mean different things for players, but all dream of winning the Grand Slam, which is achieved by winning the championship titles for all four major tennis tournaments—the Australian Open, French Open, Wimbledon, and U.S. Open—in one year.

The Australian Open was first held in Melbourne in 1905 and was subsequently hosted by other cities in Australia until 1972. Since then it has been played in the National Tennis Centre at Flinders Park in Melbourne. The Centre has a hard-court surface and the court where finals matches are played—center court—is in a 15,000-seat, retractable-roof stadium. In 1996, the Australian Open became the last of the four Grand Slam tournaments to allow amateurs and professionals to compete together. The rise in prize money at the Australian Open is an indicator of how the sport of tennis has grown: the original prize at this tournament was $5,000 for the men and $1,500 for the women. By the end of the 1990s, winners of the Australian Open earned more than $300,000.

The French Open is a nationally observed event that takes place every May in France. The court at Stade

Roland Garros, outside Paris, is made of a unique red clay. The stadium, built in 1928, seats 10,000 and is the championship's permanent home. This tournament is like no other Grand Slam because of the court playing surface—it is the only major tennis tournament played on clay. During play the red soil completely covers the players' white shoes and tennis balls. The French Open championships date back to 1891, when they were exclusively for French players. They have been open to competitors from other countries since 1925. The tournament was the first of the four Grand Slam events to open its courts to both amateurs and pros. Original prize money totaled $25,000. By the end of the century, it had reached more than $10 million. Interestingly, during World War II, both the Australian Open and Wimbledon games did not take place. However, the French got permission from the Nazi government of Germany, which then occupied the country, to resume the games in 1942. Foreigners did not compete there again until after the war, in 1946.

In June, tennis fans know it's time for Wimbledon. Although technically only the championships of Great Britain, many consider Wimbledon to be a sacred event. Since 1877, the game has been played on the grounds of the All-England Lawn Tennis and Croquet Club, more commonly known as Wimbledon, on the outskirts of London. The surface, unique to the four major tournaments, has always been grass. Wimbledon's first famed "centre court" held about 4,500 spectators; today it holds about 13,000. The tournament opened to amateurs and professionals in 1968, and prize money has escalated for singles events from a first prize of less than $5,000 for men and about $1,800 for women to over $600,000 for men and over $500,000 for women by the end of the 1990s. Wimbledon is the only Grand Slam tournament that still holds its players to a dress code of all-white clothing.

Since 1978, the U.S. Open has been played in September

A spectator's view of Center Court at Roland Garros, the site of the French Open. This Grand Slam tournament held every May is famous for its red clay surface.

in Flushing Meadow, which is located in the borough of Queens of New York City. This tournament ends the professional yearly circuit. In previous years, the Open was played at Forest Hills, Queens, at the West Side Tennis Club. The stadium opened in 1923 with a match between Great Britain and the United States. Until 1997, the center court was called the Louis Armstrong Stadium, and it seated 19,500. Today's center court is named after Arthur Ashe, the great African-American tennis player who died of AIDS in 1993. With a hard playing surface (asphalt composition), it seats 23,500 and is the largest tennis arena in the world. The U.S. Open is America's premier tennis championship.

These are the places Monica Seles dreamed of as a young teenager. But in 1986 the pro circuit was still a dream away, and life settled down to a routine in her new country. She filled her day with classes and six hours of practice, with family walks and talks sandwiched in between. Through it all, Monica never felt that her mother and father were the stereotypical obsessed tennis parents. They were a family with love as its key ingredient.

During her early tennis days in Bradenton, Florida, Monica became good friends with men's tennis star Andre Agassi (left). Both players shared the renowned Nick Bollettieri as their coach.

3

AMATEUR STATUS

MONICA'S FAMILY WAS now with her in America, but they couldn't follow her onto the court—there, she was on her own. Now she had to settle down and develop her talent.

The first time Coach Bollettieri had seen Monica play, he had been impressed by the power of her strokes. Shortly after she arrived at the academy, she spent some time practicing with another student, Jim Courier. He would turn pro in 1988 and reach the top U.S. ranking in 1991 and 1992. Another two-handed backhander, the six-foot, one-inch Courier from Florida was also impressed with young Seles. Actually, she annoyed her male opponent: Seles kept sending his shots back over the net so regularly that Courier eventually said he didn't want to play with her anymore.

It didn't matter who was on the other side of the net—Seles's love for the game kept her on the practice courts day after day. She became stronger, more sure of herself, more able to place the ball exactly where she wanted it. And all the hard work paid off. In March 1988, a 14-year-old Monica Seles was ready to join the tennis tour as an amateur.

Monica's debut performance was at the Virginia Slims tournament in Boca Raton, Florida. Her first opponent was Helen Kelesi. Seles recalled later how she was a bundle of nerves at the event. It was her first match on the tour and Kelesi was a tough player. But what really made Seles nervous was that during the second set, she spied the renowned tennis player Chris Evert watching her from the stands.

Christine Marie Evert was one of the greats of the tennis world. Born in Fort Lauderdale, Florida, in 1954, she grew up displaying a powerful two-fisted backhand that her father, also her coach, insisted she should not use. "She started to swing that way because she was too small and weak to swing the backhand with one hand," he said. The rest of the sports world got an idea of what was coming in 1970 when 15-year-old Evert stepped on the court at a minor tournament in North Carolina and defeated the number one player in the world at the time, Australia's Margaret Smith Court. At age 17, Evert made it to the semifinals of the U.S. Open, where she lost to Billie Jean King. From then on, she only climbed higher.

Evert's career would last 20 years. During its course, she would win nearly $9 million in prize money and 157 pro singles titles. Her friendly feuds with Australia's Evonne Goolagong and Czechoslovakia's Martina Navratilova over the years produced some of the decades' most exciting moments in women's tennis. Overall, Evert won 18 major titles—the Australian Open twice, the French Open seven times, Wimbledon three times, and the U.S. Open six times. The superstar, who would rank in the U.S. Top Ten for 17 years until her retirement in 1989, also kept the two-handed approach for her deadly backhand.

Evert was in the stands that day in 1988 because she was scheduled to play the winner of the Seles-Kelesi match. Seles won in two sets, but all she could think of was that she was about to play the great Chris Evert on the following evening.

That night, with shaky knees, Seles walked out on the court to battle the poker-faced, amazingly consistent Evert. Seles lost in two sets, but she did manage to win three games from the star and generally felt pretty good about her performance. It was a fine beginning.

The young talented athlete had started the long battle to the top. Few realize the difficulty in attaining the highest rungs of the tennis ladder, and especially having to do so in a foreign land. Although Seles had been to the United States a number of times before she and her family settled permanently, visiting a country and living there are two entirely different things. Her most vivid recollections of the early tournaments in Florida were taking trips to Disney World and adding to her collection of stuffed animals. She said of those early times, "I was aware of the differences in the two countries, and I still am. No matter what happens to me, I don't want to forget where I came from or behave differently with my friends."

Interestingly enough, in her new life in the United States Monica Seles *was* behaving differently, although perhaps not with her friends. She was establishing her own personality on and off the tennis court. She was proving to be an outgoing, at times bubbly young woman, given to a flair for showmanship with a ready smile or frown. At times during her career, this self-promotion would draw criticism from her opponents, but her strong will helped her face such critics without changing. Early on, she established herself as a relentless player on the court. Eventually, women players—and some of the men—at the academy wouldn't even want to practice hitting with her.

Seles spent a year on the tennis tour as an amateur. There were a lot of adjustments to make. One of them was dealing with her rapid growth. From 1988 until 1990, she went from five feet, three inches tall to five feet, nine inches. She complained that the net always seemed to be a different height. One reporter said she looked like an "animated matchstick," frantically using her racket to cut down everything in front of her.

During this time, the life of the entire Seles family became centered on Monica's career. This is not an unusual undertaking for a family that has a potential moneymaker in its ranks. Her father continued to coach her, and Zoltan became her business manager and hitting partner. There were early signs, however,

Nick Bollettieri, who in 1986 invited Monica to his tennis academy in Florida, also taught tennis greats Jim Courier, Jennifer Capriati, and Mary Pierce.

of trouble with Bollettieri. Seles would later leave the academy in a well-publicized disagreement, but for the time being she merely complained that the coach was not giving her enough of his time. Bollettieri angrily denied the accusation.

After about a year, in early 1989, Seles faced a decision. Should she remain an amateur or turn professional? In tennis, "professional" was considered to be a dirty word until the advent of the open era, when both amateurs and pros were allowed in the same tournaments and the prize money soared. And there was always the problem at the Olympic Games, for instance, when state-supported players, such as those from the former Soviet Union, were called amateurs but were actually more like professionals. They were only amateurs in name. Most were allowed to keep their prize money, although Russian athletes had to turn their winnings over to the government and were paid a salary. That practice stopped in 1990 when Soviet tennis pro Andrei Chesnokov and others made a public protest. Today, Russian professionals, like others, keep their winnings.

Every athlete at some time must decide on the right course for his or her career. In sports like football and basketball, the course is basically chosen for the athlete. It is very nearly impossible to enter the worlds of professional football or basketball without at least some college experience. That is not necessarily the case in tennis, although many players do come out of the college ranks today. But since a professional tennis career can be relatively short, there is always the perceived need to "start early." Therefore, most hopefuls choose the path of the professional early on.

Monica considered her options. If she remained an amateur, she would be eligible for a college scholarship, which interested her. If she turned pro, the opportunity to win a scholarship was gone. However, if she was successful as a pro, she could make a good deal of money. Not only would that make her own life more enjoyable, but it would also allow her to repay her family for the sacrifices they had made.

She was aware that a career in tennis, as in any sport, is risky. Time after time, young athletes have pinned their hearts on a big-time career, hoping for fame and fortune. And, if they're good enough, many of them do find success. But many times, the pro career ends because of a damaged knee or ankle, a pulled tendon, or a fractured wrist. Dreams of fame and fortune can vanish in just a few minutes.

After much consideration, Monica decided that it was time to turn pro. She figured that if she was good and won often enough, she could find a good life for her family and herself. But she also knew that the challenges ahead wouldn't be small. Nevertheless, in February 1989, the 15-year-old with the powerful strokes from that parking lot of Novi Sad entered the big-time world of professional tennis.

After attaining professional status in 1991, Monica enjoyed big prizes along with better competition. Here, Monica poses on top of a 1991 Jaguar convertible, awarded to her for capturing the top spot in the tennis rankings.

4

GOING PRO

IF YOU WANT to make it big in tennis, you want to play on center court—the main court in any tennis complex, and the court where the best players are usually scheduled to compete. When Monica Seles decided to enter the world of professional tennis, her eye was on center court from the start.

Monica's first professional match was at the Virginia Slims competition in Washington, D.C., held in February 1989. She had little trouble defeating her first two opponents and making her way to the quarter-finals. (The eight finalists compete in the quarterfinals, with the four winners meeting for the semifinals, and those two winners competing in the finals.) In the quarterfinals, Monica met Manuela Maleeva, one of three tennis-playing sisters from Bulgaria. Maleeva was ranked number nine in the world at the time. Seles was ranked a rather unimpressive 88.

It was a tough match. Seles fought hard and won the first set, 6–2. But during the second set, she sprained her ankle. This was the first of many sprains and other injuries that would plague her career. But at this first occurrence, she had a decision to make—withdraw, or play through the pain and risk further injury. Because it was her first professional match, Seles decided to play through the pain. However, she knew that if she did not win the second set, and therefore the match, she would have to withdraw. She could not endure three long sets on her damaged ankle.

Seles took the second set, 6–4, and the match. She had achieved an upset in her first competition! Now, she was slated to face the sixth ranked player in the world, American Zina Garrison, in the semifinals.

Making the semifinals was the good news. The bad news was that she had to withdraw—or, as it is called in tennis—"default." Monica told the organizers, "I'm fifteen years old, and I'm sorry, but I'm not going to play on a hurt ankle. I want to play, but I'm sorry . . . I can't—it's not worth it."

Nobody was happy with the decision, especially the tournament directors. When a player withdraws from a match, especially the semifinals or finals of a tournament, the sponsors lose spectators and money. Seles wasn't happy with the decision either. She had just begun and was excited about her entry into the world of professional tennis. But she also didn't want to risk permanent injury to her ankle.

With some rest time, Seles was ready for her next challenge—the Virginia Slims tournament in Houston, Texas, in late April. After a rather easy swing through the first rounds, she reached the semifinals to face an old opponent, Carrie Cunningham. Seles had played Cunningham twice before, winning once and losing once. But at their last meeting, when Seles was at the academy, Cunningham had trounced her, 6–1, 6–0. Seles still remembered that loss even though it had been two years before. Determined to avenge the defeat, Seles played aggressively and took Cunningham, 6–0, 6–1.

Monica had made the finals, but that meant she now had to play against, of all people, the legendary Chris Evert. Dressed in a new tennis shirt for the match, a nervous but outwardly calm Monica Seles walked on the court for the finals. She lost the first set, 6–3. But, instead of feeling crushed, she recalled, the loss seemed to strengthen her game. She was determined not to go down without a fight and bounced back by winning the second set, 6–1.

The match was even. Now she knew it was possible to beat Evert. And she did it, winning the final set, 6–4. For the rest of her career, Seles would remember that victory— her first professional championship. With a check for more money than she had ever dreamed of winning—$50,000— she and her father flew back to Florida.

The 1989 French Open was coming up, Monica's first Grand Slam event. In effect, this was the opportunity for many tennis fans to get a first look at the promising new star. Since she had joined the women's tour, many had taken notice of the strength and talent of the young girl with the two-fisted shots. She was rumored to be the one to watch.

Seles wanted to make sure that tennis fans noticed her, so she asked her mother if she could dye her hair blonde. Mrs. Seles was horrified at the thought and told her daughter she'd have to wait until she was 18 years old. But since Zoltan was with her at the French Open and not her mother, Seles had her freedom. She arrived at the stadium with strawberry-blonde hair and wearing a tennis outfit she had designed herself.

Monica was thrilled to participate at the event. She recalled the tournament in her autobiography: "The French Open at Roland Garros Stadium and Wimbledon were the only Grand Slam tournaments I used to watch on television back home. They were the stadiums I knew as a child, and the ones I fantasized about. The day I arrived in Paris I went to see the stadium. It was empty, and I climbed high into the stands and sat down; I must have been there for at least an hour, getting the feel of the place, wondering what it would be like to play there, hoping that I'd make it to the quarters or semifinals. I remember it was quiet, almost reverent there. . . . 'Maybe one day I'll win this tournament,' I whispered into the silence."

Now Monica had the chance to fulfill her wish, and she played extremely well at the French Open. After making it past the first two rounds, she found out that she was matched against Zina Garrison. Seles described what happened before that match: "I took a deep breath and walked down the corridor that led to center court. As I walked, two little girls who were friends of my parents handed me a bouquet of red roses. I entered the stadium with my arms full of roses, my ears ringing with the cheers of spectators, and my heart pounding in anticipation. I turned and tossed the roses to some fans—I couldn't really keep them on court with me, and thought the gesture would be nice."

It seemed that the tennis world had found not only a formidable talent but a bit of a showman as well. Her opponent, Zina Garrison, was not amused at Monica's dress or her attitude, nor were some of the more conventional tennis fans. But many loved the exuberance of the teenager and encouraged her style. In any event, it was evident that Monica Seles, headed for center court, was going to be herself.

Seles settled down to the task before her—beating a ranked and very tough opponent in Zina Garrison. Seles hoped that the red clay of Roland Garros, one of her favorite surfaces, would favor her, and it did. Seles won the hard-fought contest, 6–3, 6–2. At the press conference after the match, however, she was somewhat surprised to find that the reporters were more interested in why she had thrown roses into the stands than in how she had managed to overcome Garrison.

There were three more matches to go to reach the impossible dream of making the finals in her first Grand Slam event. She defeated both Jo-Anne Faull and then Manuela Maleeva, 6–3, 7–5, in the quarterfinals. She was on her way to the semifinals against the great champion, Steffi Graf, who was going for her sixth Grand Slam title.

Seles lost the first set, 6–3, but she had managed to win three games against the champion. Then she took the second set by the same score. Seles began to gain some confidence. In the third set she actually had Graf tied at three games each, but that's as close as it came. Although Seles played well, she lost the third set, 6–3. Nevertheless, it had been a terrific showing for the newcomer.

There would be two more Grand Slam tournaments for Seles during her rookie year in professional tennis. Her debut on the grass courts of Wimbledon brought her a fourth round defeat against Graf again. But she was gracious in defeat, overwhelmed with the rare chance to play at Wimbledon, and knowing that in the stands Princess Diana had watched her performance.

After the Wimbledon tournament, Seles and her family returned to their homeland for a visit, and she rejoined the tour in time for the U.S. Open beginning that August. There she reached the fourth round and once again faced Chris Evert.

Chris Evert (left) and Monica wait to begin a U.S. Open match in 1989, the last of Evert's career. Now a tennis legend, Evert was one of Monica's first major challenges.

The match received a good deal of media attention. It was Seles's first U.S. Open and Evert's last. She had just announced her retirement. The sports pages referred to the match as "passing the torch"—out goes one of the greatest players ever, and in comes a new superstar.

Monica admitted later that she was rattled when she stepped out on center court to face Chris Evert: "The crowds, the noise, the excitement of playing on center court were overwhelming. Chris Evert had the experience to tune all of those things out and play her game. She's a very steady back-court player, hardly ever misses her backhand, and hits close to the lines. That day Chris beat me, 6–0, 6–2. Someday, I thought as I walked off the court, I'll learn how to tune everything out but the game."

Still, during her first year on the pro women's tennis tour, Seles had had an incredible performance. Although she played in only three major tournaments, in a short period of time, she had made a name for herself, and had achieved a sixth-seed ranking.

But Monica had become well-known not only because of her obvious talent and strong personality. The sounds she made while she played also drew attention. While watching Seles play for a game or two, the audience becomes acutely aware of a strange, loud, grunting-like noise coming from one side of the net—most notably after a serve. And the sound is quite audible; even fans watching on television can hear it.

Some people—most usually her opponents—find the grunting noise terribly distracting and annoying. But Seles says she doesn't do it to be annoying; she doesn't do it to be anything. "My grunts have always been a natural way to release air and energy. Any athlete who exerts momentary bursts of physical effort has to release the air in her lungs," she explains. "It just happens from all the effort of cracking the ball over the net."

In 1990, Seles split with coach Nick Bollettieri. She thought he was spending more time on the career of Andre Agassi than her own. The family moved to a home in Sarasota, Florida, and Monica found herself practicing on public courts once again with her father as her only coach. That year she ran up a string of 36 victories, which was finally ended by Zina Garrison at Wimbledon. Later, in Berlin, Seles ended Steffi Graf's 66-match winning streak.

All in all, Monica won nine titles in 1990 and ended the year ranked number two. She defeated Steffi Graf for her

first Grand Slam title at the French Open that year, where she became the youngest player to win a singles competition in 103 years. It was an exhilarating win for her. She later said, "Grand Slam titles are very special to tennis players: they put you up with the very few at the top. It's a kind of rite of passage—winning the French Open told me that I'd finally made it. I no longer had to wonder whether I was good enough, or chalk up my wins to luck. I had made it, and nobody could take that away from me."

Monica also won the Most Improved Player award from the Women's Tennis Association (WTA) in 1990. Her prize

During most of the 1990s, Monica had a long-standing rivalry with German star Steffi Graf. In 1989, the players faced each other during two Grand Slams—the French Open and Wimbledon.

earnings that season totaled more than $1.6 million. But she also made another $6 million in endorsement contracts, appearances fees, and modeling contracts, having quickly become a sports celebrity. Monica would ultimately model for *Vogue*, *Elle*, and *Seventeen* magazines.

Things continued to look up for Monica, with 1991 proving to be a spectacular year. Seles reached the finals in all 16 of the tournaments that she entered, beginning in January with the Australian Open, played in 134-degree heat. The night after that first match, Seles found the soles of her feet were blistered and burned. With a finals win against Jana Novotna in the relative coolness of 104 degrees, Seles became the youngest winner of the Australian Open at the age of 17 years, two months. She was just four months younger than Margaret Smith had been when she won the Australian Open in 1960.

By March, Seles had knocked Graf out of the number one spot in women's tennis. In doing so, she became the youngest player ever to reach that rank; America's Tracy Austin had been one month older when she set the record in 1979. Still, as Monica explained in her autobiography, "Being number one was never my goal, but once I was there I wasn't eager to have it taken away."

Seles took the French and U.S. Opens that year, too, but she missed out on achieving the coveted Grand Slam due to some misfortune at Wimbledon. She didn't lose at the tournament—she never even participated, having unexpectedly withdrawn from the tournament about 72 hours before the games began—amid much media hype and controversy.

Seles explained her absence from the tournament at first by claiming that she had been injured in a minor accident, but later said that she withdrew from Wimbledon because she had developed shin splints from jogging on pavement and had been advised by her doctor to rest. "I was torn. I really wanted to play Wimbledon," Monica later explained. "I had a shot at joining Steffi Graf to

After losing to Steffi Graf in the French Open semifinals in 1989, Monica returned the following year to defeat her in the finals and win her first Grand Slam title.

become the second female Grand Slam title winner in three years. Only a handful of women in the history of the sport have ever had that honor. But physically, I knew I couldn't play."

But Monica had not informed the press about her reasons for withdrawing from the tournament. Instead, she had just disappeared, first returning home to Florida to rest, and then later entering a rehabilitation clinic in Vail, Colorado, for physical therapy.

Rumors quickly began to circulate about the cause of Monica's absence from Wimbledon. One rumor was that one of her sponsors was paying her a million dollars *not* to play at the major tournament. As a result of her disappearance, Seles received a great deal of criticism from the media as well as from other players.

Seles compounded the mess by agreeing to play in an exhibition tournament—the Pathmark Tennis Classic—in Mahwah, New Jersey, only a week after Wimbledon. It didn't help that she attended the press conference given by the tournament's promoter and held up the T-shirt he gave her. It displayed the words, "Rome, Paris, Wimbledon, Mahwah"—with Wimbledon crossed out.

Seles later admitted that she had made some bad judgments about the way she had handled the withdrawal from Wimbledon. But she insisted she had no reason not to go to a tournament that could have given her the Grand Slam title if she wasn't really hurt.

Monica's fans eventually forgave her for not taking part in Wimbledon in 1991, but the press never really did. The WTA fined her $6,000 for pulling out of the tournament without notice or proof of any injury. And for playing in a non-tour event, she was fined another $20,000 for taking part in the Mahwah exhibition tournament.

By the end of July, Seles had returned to the women's tour. In September, she won her first U.S. Open. She won three out of four Grand Slams in 1991, ending the year still holding on to her number one ranking. She was also honored as the WTA singles player of the year and the youngest ever to be the World Champion. She had earned more than $2.4 million from tournaments.

Things promised to get even better in 1992. Monica took her second straight Australian Open, beating Mary Joe Fernandez, 6–2, 6–3, in the finals. Steffi Graf was absent this time with the German measles. Still, Seles got

In 1991 Monica abruptly announced she would not play at Wimbledon. She sparked controversy by appearing just a week later at an exhibition tournament in Mahwah, New Jersey, where she held up a T-shirt displaying the words "Rome, Paris, Wimbledon, Mahwah"—with Wimbledon crossed out.

the opportunity to play against Graf in the French Open, where Monica became the first woman to win the event three times in a row since Hilde Sperling did it in 1937. The difficult match took two hours and 43 minutes, but Seles beat Graf, 6–2, 3–6, 10–8. Afterward, Monica said, "This is the hardest I've ever had to work for a Grand Slam title."

It looked like Seles really was on track for the Grand

Slam. But the elusive prize eluded her again in June at Wimbledon. Some say that Seles caused herself to lose Wimbledon that year. Complaints were coming in from all quarters about her infamous grunting during a match. The tabloid press got wind of it and fanned the flames. During the semifinals even Martina Navratilova complained about the grunts to the umpire, saying, "It just gets loud and louder. You cannot hear the ball being hit."

No one will ever know whether Seles caved under the pressure in the finals, but she didn't utter one grunt during the entire match. She explained why in her autobiography: "I decided to change: I would hold my breath in after I hit the ball instead of exhaling with the force. When I stepped onto center court to play Steffi Graf in the Wimbledon finals, I only thought about one thing: Don't grunt. It was one of the biggest mistakes I've ever made."

Graf took the tournament, 6–2, 6–1.

For the rest of the year, Monica continued to make an effort to control her grunting, hoping to stave off the accusations that she won some matches unfairly. And, except for her defeat at Wimbledon, Seles seemed invincible, taking the U.S. Open over Arantxa Sanchez-Vicario. In all, Seles was beaten just five times in 1992 and won 10 titles. Her victory in Barcelona that year, at age 18 years and 4 months, made her the youngest player ever to win 25 singles titles, surpassing Tracy Austin's record of 18 years and 8 months.

At the end of 1992 Seles was voted Player of the Year for the second straight time. She also beat out Stefan Edberg's prize money record for one season, having earned $2.6 million dollars in tour prizes that year.

With the coming of the new season for 1993, Seles was surely the player to beat. Many fans believed 1993 was the year for Seles to take the Grand Slam. And it started off well. After a two-month rest, Monica was once more back at the Australian Open, facing Steffi

Graf. She won, 4–6, 6–3, 6–2, chalking up three titles and 21 consecutive matches won. However, soon after the event she came down with a viral infection, which sidelined her for several weeks until she felt well enough to enter a tournament in Hamburg, Germany. That event would bring her fairy-tale tennis life crashing down around her.

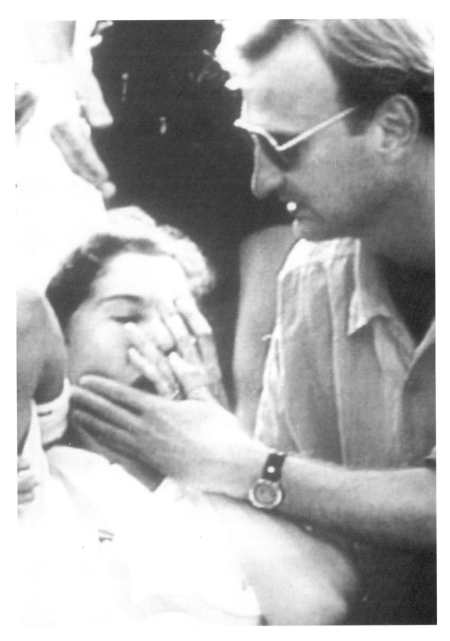

A stunned Monica receives emergency treatment after being stabbed in the back at a 1993 tournament in Hamburg, Germany.

5

"TERROR AND PAIN"

TODAY, SPECTATORS AT professional tennis matches, whether indoors at New York's Madison Square Garden or outdoors at England's Wimbledon, will immediately notice the guards on the courts. They look like ushers, and at times they will play that role. However, they also have another job: each time the tennis players come off the court to sit down during breaks between games, the ushers must stand behind them. They are not there to give the players privacy—the guards are there instead to keep the tennis players separate from the spectators, or more precisely, to keep any over-zealous or even crazed spectator from getting to the tennis players. This security measure stems from what happened to Monica Seles in 1993. It was not only a terrifying incident; it also very nearly ended her career.

It was April 30—a sunny, crisp day in Hamburg, Germany. Seles, the world's number one–ranked female tennis player at the time, had reached the quarterfinals in the Citizen Cup tournament. In the next round she would play the heavy hitting Magdalena Maleeva at 5 P.M. One of three tennis-playing sisters from Bulgaria, Maleeva was a budding star on the tennis circuit. She had won her first pro title in 1992 and would reach her highest world rank of sixth in 1995. Both sisters had also risen that high—Manuela in 1984 and 1988, and Katerina in 1990.

Seles had mixed feelings about this tournament. Part of her was thrilled because her family, including her brother Zoltan, was there, and he had been hitting with her on the courts before the tournament. However, she was concerned about her health. Due to a virus she contracted, she had hardly played at all during the month of March and most of April. She still felt weak. In fact, the reason she had entered the Hamburg tournament was to build up some strength so she could be in shape for the upcoming French Open in June.

Seles was also concerned about something else. For some time now, she had been dismayed about her own safety. Most of that concern stemmed from the fighting taking place in her homeland of the former Yugoslavia. The hatred and violence exhibited between Serbs and Croats was especially vicious and was continually increasing. Although her family was ethnic Hungarian, she had received death threats from Croats because of her Serbian origins. One such threat had come at Wimbledon the year before, just before her match with champion Martina Navratilova.

There had also been some unpleasant incidents in which people in tennis stadiums had aggressively pushed their way to get to her. And at least one time, on the way to her hotel after a match, her driver thought they were being followed. Monica had begun wearing wigs and changing the style of her clothes to disguise herself in public. Sometimes she would make duplicate plane reservations as well.

As a celebrity, Monica had every right to fear stalkers.

However, usually the price that celebrities pay for being famous is the occasional annoyance of people asking for autographs or interrupting a private dinner in a restaurant. But sometimes the price is worse. Sometimes celebrities like Monica receive threats to their own lives.

On that April day in 1993, with her usual worries about the fans and her game, Seles walked onto the court for her quarterfinals match against Maleeva. The first set was tough, but Seles managed to pull it out with a win, 6–4. However, the chilly weather and her own fatigue hindered her playing during the second set, and she lost the first three games. There was no hope of looking into the stands for encouragement that afternoon, however. Her father had apparently come down with the same virus she had, and he and her mother were resting back at the hotel. Zoltan had said he would come along during the match, but Monica hadn't seen him yet in the stands.

Monica knew that if she was going to win the match, she had to do it soon. If it went on much longer, the match would have to be postponed until the next day due to darkness. In that case, if she managed to win she would have to play the semifinal match on the same day she finished this one. In her weakened condition, that didn't seem like a good idea.

So, Seles got back on the court and fought. She brought the second set to a tie, 3–3, and then went ahead, 4–3. At the changeover—a one-minute break taken when players change sides—Monica knew she needed to take just two more games to win the set and the match.

Seles and Maleewa walked to the sidelines and sat down on chairs, with their backs to the crowd of nearly 10,000 spectators. Seles threw a towel over her head and concentrated on how she would win those two games.

Suddenly, Monica felt a sharp burning pain in her

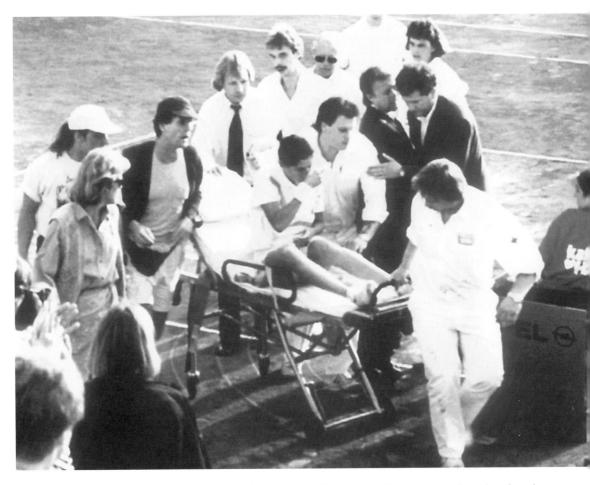

Minutes after the attack, medics wheel Monica off the court and take her to a nearby hospital, where she would recover during the next three days.

back and down her right side. She screamed and twisted her head back, straining to look over her left shoulder. What she saw, in horror, was a man in a baseball cap holding a nine-inch-long curved, bloody knife. It was a man she had seen earlier at the practice courts and at the hotel. He lifted the knife as if to stab her again.

But before the assailant could strike, a security guard grabbed the man and wrestled him to the ground. One of the spectators rushed forward to help Monica as she struggled to stand, then fell in a daze to the court, dizzy with pain and fear. She was having trouble breathing. Trainer Madeleine Van Zoelen rushed to the stricken tennis star. Monica recalled, "I asked her what had happened, but couldn't hear her reply over the drumming in my ears. Everything was happening too fast for my mind to catch up."

Then, suddenly Zoltan was at her side. From the stands, he had seen the attack and rushed out on the court. Monica remembered how relieved she was to see him: "I didn't ask any questions after I saw Zoltan. I knew he'd take care of me."

Although to Seles it seemed that hours went by, in just a few minutes a stretcher arrived, and she was wheeled off the court and into an ambulance, which rushed her to the nearby hospital. Zoltan went with her. By the time they reached the emergency room, Monica's parents had arrived. But she was still frantic. "[E]verything came in flashes of terror and pain," she would explain later.

Doctors cleaned the wound—the cut had damaged the soft tissues and muscles by the scapula, or shoulder blade. The wound was one and a half inches deep, and located just next to her spine. Monica's doctors told her she was lucky. Had the blade hit her spine, she could have been paralyzed.

But Seles didn't feel so lucky. She was overcome with fear and pain, concerned that the assailant would come back. Even the guards posted at her hospital door did not reassure her. The fear would not go away. Only the presence of her family helped her feel safe until some medication relaxed her enough for sleep.

In her autobiography, Monica recalled how she agonized over what had happened: "Just yesterday I was focused on the French Open, I thought in amazement as I lay in my hospital bed. I was sure that I had a good chance of defending my Grand Slam title and maybe of becoming the first player in the world to win four consecutive French Open Championships. Just yesterday I was the undeniable number one player in the world. Now everything had changed. I was no longer the strong person I had been twenty-four hours previously."

That day German tennis star Steffi Graf showed up in Seles's hospital room. She tried to apologize for the violent attack that had taken place in her home country, but both young women just cried.

Later, Monica was disturbed to learn that the Citizen Cup tournament had continued without her. Many supporters gathered outside her hospital window in protest of the decision to continue the tournament despite the attack on one of its participants. Monica later noted that she was disappointed that players participated in the event, despite everything that had happened.

After a three-day stay in the hospital, Monica flew back to the United States for more tests and treatment at the Steadman Hawkins Clinic in Vail, Colorado. By that time, she had learned the identity of her attacker. Strangely enough, after all the fears she had resulting from the unrest in her homeland, Monica learned that her assailant had nothing to do with Yugoslavia at all. His name was Günther Parche, and he was an unemployed German machinist. His reason for the attack was that he was in love—not with Monica Seles, but with Steffi Graf, the great German champion whom Seles had knocked out of the number one spot into number two. Using his misguided reasoning, Parche had decided to take Seles out of the game, thus making Graf number one once again.

Just how bizarre Parche's reasoning was became evident in some statements from his testimony to the German police after his attack on Seles. He explained, "I am a great fan of Steffi Graf. . . . [I]n 1990 Steffi Graf lost to Monica Seles in the German Open in Berlin. My world collapsed around me at that time. I could not bear the thought of someone beating Steffi Graf."

Later in his confession, the obsessed fan explained how he wanted to injure Monica so she could not beat

Joined by her doctor, Robert Steadman, Monica describes her injury to the press at a medical center in Vail, Colorado.

his adored Steffi Graf again: "I noticed how relatively easy it is to walk along the first row and get behind Monica Seles. I had already thought through various means of getting to Seles. . . . This act [of stabbing her] was her punishment for the past three years. It really upset me that Monica Seles was above Steffi Graf in the world tennis ranking."

Parche's violent act would have drastic, long-term consequences for his victim.

Monica takes a minute to compose herself during a press conference several days after the stabbing in Hamburg, Germany. Monica's recovery from the attack would be her greatest challenge, and it would keep her away from the tennis court for two years.

6

THE DARKNESS
OF DEPRESSION

MONICA'S WOUND WAS not life threatening and would heal quickly. But Monica had been hurt in another way—her mental well-being had been devastated. Right after the attack, while in the hospital, an intense fear had gripped her. She would wake in the safety of her hospital bed and call for Zoltan or her parents, afraid somehow that Parche or some other assailant would get to her. Even knowing that Hamburg police patrolled the hospital hallways did not help. No amount of reassurance could take away that anxiety. This kind of reaction is not at all unusual for a trauma victim.

Then, a few days after the attack, Seles received a blow of a different nature, but almost as devastating. The Women's Tennis Association met in Rome to discuss what to do about her ranking. She was the best in women's tennis, number one in the world. But it was obvious that she wasn't going to be able to defend that ranking—at least for a while. And two of the big Grand Slam tournaments were coming up—the French Open in late May, followed by the prestigious Wimbledon.

At the meeting, which included 17 of the 25 top-ranked women's players, the head of the WTA, Gerard Smith, asked that Seles's ranking be locked in, or frozen, until she returned to the courts. However, the voting players—including Steffi Graf—said no. That meant if Graf won the upcoming French Open, she would once again be number one, which is exactly what happened. It began to look like Günther Parche had helped Monica's competition after all.

At the time, however, Seles was more concerned with her return to the United States. When the plane landed in Denver, Colorado, she was eager to undergo the final leg of the long journey to reach the Steadman Hawkins Clinic. She had confidence in the two orthopedic surgeons who ran the physical therapy institute, having been there in 1991 for the rehabilitation of a shin injury. This time her stay was expected to be about two months—it lasted six.

Sometimes, a person's emotions during a crisis can be like a volcano. It may seem peaceful and calm on the outside, but can one day erupt and nearly tear itself apart. At first, Monica seemed calm. Putting aside the fear about the stabbing and the hurt over the WTA's decision regarding her ranking, she instead concentrated on getting her body back into shape.

But Monica still knew that the assault had affected her deeply. During the month of May she became more removed, more distant, taking off by herself or with her mother for drives through the Colorado mountains. The month of June found her doing more of the same—driving for hours with no destination in mind. She would break down into tears, suffer from nightmares, and have trouble getting out of bed in the morning.

Finally Seles's doctors recommended that she see a clinical psychologist, Dr. Jerry Russel May. In July Monica flew to his offices in Lake Tahoe, California, for a ten-day session. But, she admitted later that she was not able to open up to him about her problems at that time. Dr. May encouraged her, and offered his help whenever she was ready to accept it. In her autobiography, Monica admits that she just couldn't tell him what troubled her: "I couldn't say that I was unable to imagine myself walking out on a tennis court again, sitting with my back to the spectators; that I was afraid my career was over. The words just wouldn't come out."

Meanwhile the media persisted in getting an explanation for Monica's continued absence from the women's tennis tour. In August, she agreed to an interview with ABC journalist Diane Sawyer. The interview proved very difficult, with Monica breaking down into tears during the taping, but she managed to finish it. After it aired, the pressure from the media lessened a bit.

In September, Monica began working out with the great track and field star Jackie Joyner-Kersee and her husband, famed coach Bobby Kersee. For the next ten weeks of this training, she began to feel pretty good. By October, Monica had managed to return to the tennis court, hitting balls lobbed to her by her father. As she explained, "It just happened—we didn't plan it. . . . I had to do something to quiet the voices in my head—the ones that said [Günther Parche] was going to hurt me again; the ones that screamed in the night."

Physical exertion seemed to work. Because she was so tired from running several miles and lifting weights each morning, followed by an afternoon of working with her father, most of Monica's nights were dreamless. She began to think that it might be possible to play in the Australian Open the following January—that maybe it would be possible to get back that number one ranking after all.

But in October, Monica received word that the man responsible for so much torment in her life had received a light sentence. When he had confessed to police, Parche had stated, "I think I will probably get fifteen years' imprisonment." Actually, Parche didn't even get one year. He was tried on a charge of bodily injury rather than attempted murder because he had stated that he wanted to wound, not kill Seles. Although he had been found guilty, his two-year sentence was suspended, and he was freed by the German courts with the order that he check in regularly with probation officers over the next two years. Seles could not believe it.

"I'd spend the next two years in the jail he was supposed to inhabit," she later said. "Two years hiding in shadows, afraid to play professional tennis, afraid to even step onto a public court." The verdict was a crush to Monica's peace of mind. Although she continued training throughout November, she couldn't sleep as well anymore.

Seles received another setback before the end of the year when her father, who had been diagnosed with prostate cancer around the time of the attack, had to undergo surgery again, this time for stomach cancer. Monica's world, complete with the love of a close-knit family and a future bright with tennis wins, was falling apart. Although she believed she had put thoughts of the stabbing behind her, the nightmares resurfaced in December, waking her at night and making her cry out in fear. She sank into a depression, no longer interested in training or tennis. "Darkness was everywhere," she described her feelings.

What Monica Seles was suffering from is called PTSD, or post-traumatic stress disorder. It's quite common in those who have suffered attacks of violence. Sometimes PTSD hits immediately after the trauma; other times, as in Seles's case, it takes longer to surface. Occasionally the victim's condition can get so bad that he or she cannot leave the house because the fear is so real. Or, as with Seles, the person tries to keep up a brave front, denying the shock, fear, depression, and anxiety that he or she feels. This tends to keep the fears regarding the trauma at bay for a while, but they generally return. And when they do, all the defenses collapse at once, and the victim collapses, too. So it was with Seles during the Christmas season of 1993.

Dr. William Nathan, noted psychiatrist with the famed

Meninger Clinic in Topeka, Kansas, spoke of PTSD in an interview for this book. "Severe trauma of many kinds may lead to PTSD," says Nathan. "Those who served in the military during wars were exposed to sights, sounds, and experiences nobody ever anticipates until they happen. These reactions were known as shell shock during World War I and as combat fatigue during World War II and the Korea War. Lots of campaigns, such as the Battle of the Bulge [a particularly bloody battle of World War II], left us with many cases of PTSD."

Many people, including Monica, felt that her assailant, Günther Parche, did not receive the punishment he deserved. Here, Parche leaves jail with his belongings only five months after the attack.

Nathan notes that the cause of PTSD is "inescapable exposure to life-threatening or massively injurious circumstances." The hallmarks of the disorder, he says, include "vivid memories, flashbacks, dreams, inability to revisit the scene or similar places or a compulsion to revisit the scene in an effort to master the trauma, recurrent images, hallucinations, numbness, anger, sleeplessness, and other problems."

As in Monica's case, with this disorder there is a feeling of having no control over your life, that the future may never happen, that life and good fortune can end at any time. For some people who are victims of violent attacks, it may be easier and less stressful to return to their job or workplaces as soon as possible, to give them the sense that their everyday life is back in order. But the idea of returning to the tennis circuit was not so easy for Seles. Her workplace left her exposed to the strangers in the stadium stands.

Seles experienced many of the symptoms noted by Dr. William Nathan. She relived the moments of the attack again and again. "My scream is what stayed with me a long time," she later said. She couldn't sleep. She couldn't face much of her life and certainly not her life in tennis. More than ever she withdrew from the spotlight that had put her in so much danger. She sank further into a sea of depression, sleeping several hours in the middle of the day, and eating uncontrollably. By the end of February she had gained 35 pounds, growing from 140 to 175 pounds.

Still, during this time, there was one event that lifted her depression. After living in the United States for eight years, Monica and her mother had decided to become American citizens. Both took and passed the citizenship test in March 1994. It was a proud day for them both, and Seles later revealed that the experience had lifted her spirits.

That same month, at her father's insistence, Seles began regular therapy sessions with the clinical psychologist she had visited the previous July—Dr. Jerry May. She spent two weeks in Lake Tahoe, California, undergoing therapy, and found she was finally able to accept his help. "I began to trust him," she said. "We started to talk about the last three months and how I'd succumbed to my depression and fears until they controlled me." She admitted to Dr. May that at this point she would be happy to recover enough so she could enjoy playing tennis again just in her own backyard.

Dr. May helped Monica understand that her symptoms were normal and that she had to learn how to control her depression, which would happen as soon as she managed to balance her emotions, behaviors, and thoughts. The physician encouraged her to set small goals, to learn how to control her fear, beginning with taking walks in her own backyard.

Back home in Sarasota, Florida, she talked to May several times a week on the phone, knowing she would return for more therapy in another five weeks. She was encouraged to talk to other trauma victims as well. Getting over PTSD is generally a long, hard process.

Monica was accompanied by her brother Zoltan for the return trip for therapy in May. At this point she could finally tell Dr. May about her biggest worry: "I couldn't visualize myself walking out on a court ever again: when I tried to imagine it, all I saw was darkness."

Dr. May encouraged her to work on controlling the nightmares and negative thoughts with conditioning and relaxation techniques. Once she mastered relaxation, he explained, she could use that technique to overcome her uneasiness. Her brother Zoltan was a great help as well, accompanying her in situations she could not handle on her own. With May's encouragement, Zoltan began taking his sister into public places—first a stop in a coffee shop, then the next week the supermarket. Little by little, these normal everyday activities helped Seles to get back some pieces of her life.

It was in Tahoe that Monica managed, with Dr. May's help, to step back on an open tennis court—one located at

Monica's brother, Zoltan, was a great support for her during the tough months following the stabbing. He assisted Monica in getting back routines of daily life as well as serving as her personal chaperone.

his country club. She played 30 minutes, then couldn't continue. Still, her therapist congratulated her on achieving this milestone.

Seles and Zoltan returned to Florida with new hopes. Monica found she could play on the court in her backyard with her brother. Finally she played her first doubles match, against her father and former pro tennis player Betsy Nagelsen, with her husband, Mark McCormack, as Monica's partner.

Overall, however, she still could not play much tennis and took up other activities to fill the void. She water-skied, played pool, and learned to play the guitar. Meanwhile she also grew another inch taller and gained some weight. She felt encouraged by the support of her friends, including tennis stars Martina Navratilova and Jennifer Capriati.

By the time of her return visit to Tahoe in June for more therapy, Monica could claim some improvements, including her renewed joy in playing tennis again. She continued to see Dr. May that summer and continued to work on setting and achieving her goals while at home. It was slow going, but she was making progress.

Monica holds a toy Kangaroo and a trophy, which she received after winning the 1996 Australian Open. It was her first Grand Slam title after her two-year absence from the professional circuit.

7

RALLY

IN THE FALL of 1994 Monica received a special gift—a devoted fan's encouragement that would urge the tennis pro on to the final steps toward recovery. The fan was a young girl, Sonya Bell, who had herself demonstrated great courage. Because of a birth defect Sonya began to lose her vision when she was two years old. By the time she was nine, she was totally blind. While attending a school for the hearing- and vision-disabled in Spartensburg, South Carolina, she took up track and roller and ice-skating. Eventually, Sonya became a gymnast, capable of somersaulting over a balance beam that she could not see and swinging from uneven bars she could only feel.

In November 1994, Seles was asked to present the Arete Award for the most courageous athlete of the year, which was to be given to 13-year-old Sonya Bell. Why Seles? Because Bell had said that Seles was her hero.

How could Monica refuse such a request? Even though she was nervous about making a public appearance for the first time in more than a year, she accepted. Along with her mother, Seles flew to Chicago for the ceremony. When she was introduced to Bell, the young gymnast said, "I watch you all the time. I know it's you because I can hear you grunting." Seles laughed. At last, someone approved of her grunts.

Later, Seles commented on how much presenting the award to Bell had helped her in overcoming her own personal fears. "Her bravery and determination were an inspiration to me," Seles explained.

That same month, another stranger would also help Seles in her struggle to get back her life. Shortly after the Chicago trip, Seles and her mother flew to Seattle, Washington, to visit a friend—the trip itself was part of Monica's therapy. Outside a store in the city, Seles met a homeless Vietnam War veteran and his dog. She began a conversation with the stranger, who told her that he had not been able to get his life back together since the war. He talked about suffering flashbacks and nightmares, symptoms with which she could readily identify. When they parted, Seles gave him money for himself and his dog. She remembered thinking at the time, "I don't want to be like that. . . . I've got to start focusing on the present, otherwise I'll be stuck in the past, too. No more 'tomorrow I'll get on the court— tomorrow I'll start exercising—tomorrow I'll stop letting Parche's actions control me.' There was only *now.* I was weeks away from my twenty-first birthday. It was time to live again."

Although it would take several more months before Monica strode back onto the courts before her public, she had taken a major step. In December she began training in earnest. One day in late February 1995, Martina Navratilova came to see her friend and to play some tennis with Monica on her backyard court. After the practice Martina took a gold bracelet off her wrist and handed it to Monica, saying, "Monica, I want you to have this. It has brought me a lot of luck." When Monica insisted she could not accept the gift, Martina replied, "When you come back, you can return it to me."

Seles said later, "Maybe it was the bracelet, or maybe it was just time to move on. I like to think it was a little bit of both."

Before her return to tennis, Seles flew to Paris while the French Open was being held, but she did not go to the tournament. Instead, she met with representatives of the Women's Tennis Association concerning her return to the game and the status of her ranking. They also talked about what new security measures would be in place on the courts.

In addition to losing her ranking during her stay away from the game, Seles had lost a major sponsor as well. In today's world, where sports are not just games but also a billion-dollar advertising business, it is common practice for companies and organizations to "sponsor" athletes. The athlete wears the recognizable company logo on his or her shirt or uniform. In return for this advertising, the athlete is paid, usually very well. In fact, many athletes earn far more from sponsors than from their playing contracts.

In Seles's case, her sponsor for some time had been Fila, an Italian manufacturer of sports clothes and sneakers. During her absence, Fila had turned out a million-dollar sports line in her name. But because she kept postponing her return to the women's tennis circuit, Fila kept losing money. An athlete out of the public eye is not selling sports clothes. So, Fila had canceled the contract.

In her autobiography, Monica explained she couldn't let concerns about money govern her actions. She had to recover first:

It's true that I had record career earnings in '91 and '92, and signed some lucrative endorsement contracts. But through it all, my parents' warnings have stayed in my ears. "Monica, remember that money comes and goes," my parents said. "You've got to be the same person regardless of whether or not you have it. Keep your feet always on the ground where they belong."

After the attack in 1993 I didn't earn any money for two years. And though there were rumors that I collected insurance money, they were untrue. I didn't collect a penny. Some of my sponsors believed in me and kept me on; some dropped me; and one decided to sue me for staying out of the game. During that year I realized more than ever that my parents had been right—and there was no guarantee I'd continue to earn money playing tennis. And the person I was, the family and friends I had, the life I'd chosen, were the only things that truly belonged to me.

With a renewed vigor, 21-year-old Seles set a date for her return to tennis in an exhibition match against Martina Navratilova—July 25, 1995. She practiced, trained, dieted, and worked out. A few weeks before the match, she appeared in New Haven, Connecticut, at the Special Olympics World Games. Understandably, Monica was nervous—it was only her second public appearance since the stabbing.

At the Special Olympics event, she met Sonya Bell once again and was greeted by Eunice Kennedy Shriver, the founder of the Special Olympics. Shriver asked Seles for a tennis lesson, and with pleasure Monica agreed. At the games, Monica handed out awards to the players and played doubles matches with some of the athletes. She remembered being impressed with "the strength and spirit . . . in the Special Olympians."

Monica knew that the upcoming match against Navratilova would be challenging not only because it required her to play before the public but also because she would face a formidable opponent. Although Martina Navratilova had retired the year before, she was still a great opponent.

Born in Prague, Czechoslovakia, in 1956, Martina Navratilova had first entered tournaments in the United States at age 16. In 1973, she lost to Chris Evert in Akron, Ohio, but Chris remembered her well. "I could tell she'd be trouble," she said later. Over the next 16 years, their rivalry

was one of the best in the game and resulted in some of the best matches ever played in women's tennis.

Fitness, quickness, and strength had been Navratilova's trademarks, and her play had often been described as awesome. Over the course of her career, she played in the most singles tournaments (380) and matches (1,650) and won the most titles (167) and matches (1,438) in women's tennis, with a won-lost record of 1,438–212. She won more prize money—over $10 million—than any other player except tennis greats Ivan Lendl and Pete Sampras. And her record in singles championships alone in the Grand Slams is mind-boggling: Australian Open, three times; French Open, twice; Wimbledon, nine times; and the U.S. Open, four

Monica demonstrates a proper forehand shot to a player at a clinic held at the 1995 Special Olympics World Games.

times. Navratilova ranked in the U.S. top ten for 14 years, never below number three. For 11 straight years, starting in 1982, she was number one.

Yet despite Navratilova's impressive record, Monica had gladly accepted the challenge for the exhibition match, where she had proved that the time was right for her return to tennis. After her win over Navratilova, Seles knew she was back where she had to be—in the world of professional tennis, where she belonged.

But there was still much work to be done. Although Monica was taller and stronger, she was also heavier. She told the press that she would not diet, however, feeling that her increased activity of practice and matches would take care of her weight.

After the July exhibition match, the Women's Tennis Association came to a new agreement on Seles's tennis ranking. She would be co-ranked with Steffi Graf as number one for the first six events in which she played, or for one year, whichever came first. This was a satisfactory agreement for Seles, but not for some of the other women tennis players, who believed that Seles had been away from the pro circuit too long to be given number one status.

But nonetheless she was number one, and her eye was now on the Canadian Open championships in Toronto, coming up that August. Seles did not have much faith in her ability to do well in Toronto. It was her first hard test, after all. More important, she had developed tendonitis in her left knee since the exhibition match. But there was little she could do for the injury except rest.

Tendonitis is an inflammation of the white fibrous cord, or tendon, that connects muscle to bone in the human body. Constant strain, as in competitive sports, can injure the tendon. The area becomes very painful and tender, and if the muscle remains active, tendonitis does not heal. Rest, of course, is the best medicine, although the injury can also be treated using support bandages, painkillers, or steroid drugs. Tendonitis is a common ailment for athletes, professional and

otherwise, and may occur almost anywhere in the body. It's most common, however, at the shoulders or heels, outside the elbows (tennis elbow), or inside the elbows (golfer's elbow).

At the Canadian Open the crowd rejoiced at seeing Monica Seles on the court again, chanting her name over and over again. While Seles was dubious about her chances at winning the tournament, her father was overjoyed just to see her on the court. He didn't care if she won, he said, just that "Monica smiles."

As it turned out, his daughter had a good deal to smile about. In rather quick fashion, she took care of her opponents. First she defeated American player Kimberly Po in 60 minutes. Next came Nathalie Tauziat of France, who Monica sent home in just 56 minutes. Then she faced Amanda Coetzer of South Africa in the finals. That took less than an hour, too. Seles won, 6–0, 6–1. *Tennis* magazine enthusiastically proclaimed, "Seles is back. And how."

Martina Navratilova (left), who maintained a closely followed rivalry with Chris Evert (right) during the 1980s, was a great mentor for Monica during her return to tennis in 1995.

As she accepted her award at the Canadian Open closing ceremony, Monica shared her thoughts with the crowd: "I can't believe this is for real. It's been such a long time and I was never sure I would ever play tennis again."

But an even bigger test was coming up—the U.S. Open in New York City. As though to forestall any disappointment, Seles kept telling everyone that she was just going to have fun in New York that August. It didn't matter how well she did at the tournament, she explained. And in fact, she did seem to be having fun. She took walks in Central Park—for the most part unnoticed by New Yorkers—saw two Broadway shows (*Showboat* and *How to Succeed in Business*), attended the New York Giants football game, and signed autographs whenever asked.

When she took to the courts at the tournament in New York, however, Monica was still bothered by the tendonitis in her left knee. She faced her first opponent—Ruxandra Dragomir of Romania—in an evening match. Despite her injury, Seles took the match, 6–3, 6–1.

The fourth round gave her a tough opponent in the German player Anke Huber. Now wearing a brace on her ailing knee, Seles took the match in two sets, 6–1, 6–4. Next came the quarterfinals with Jana Novotna. Seles needed a tie-breaker to take the first set, but won the second easily, 6–2. The semifinals pitted her against Conchita Martinez of Spain.

All Monica could think about, she later recalled, was winning as quickly as possible and getting back to the hotel to rest her aching knee before the next day's final. The match was not over until 7:30 that evening, but Seles won it, 6–2, 6–2.

The day of the finals was all a tennis fan could wish for. Number one was playing number one—Steffi Graf against Monica Seles. This was the toughest test of Monica's comeback. In the first set, which went into a tie-breaker, Seles disagreed with an umpire's call and was visibly upset when Graf took the set. Fighting to control her anger, which for her is usually not a problem, Seles won the

second set. But in the end, Graf prevailed and took the third set and match, with the final scores 7–6, 0–6, 6–4.

The two opponents met at the net and shook hands. Graf commented later that her win was minor compared to Monica Seles's courageous return to the courts: "It's even more important to see [Monica] play that well and obviously enjoy herself and be so at peace with herself. It's so great to see that." Although Monica was disappointed in her loss, she was pleased overall with her return to professional tennis. At the end of 1995 the WTA named Seles the Comeback Player of the Year.

In 1996, Seles was ready to take back the number one spot in women's tennis. And she knew that the journey would begin with the first Grand Slam of the year, the

Monica and Steffi Graf hug each other at the net after a match. Upon Monica's 1995 return to professional tennis, Monica's closest rival commended her for her courage and spirit.

Australian Open. After nursing knee and ankle injuries for most of the previous year, she felt healthy and ready to take on all challengers.

Thinking that a tune-up for the Australian Open would not hurt, Seles flew to Australia in early January 1996 to play in the Peters NSW Open. There, she reached the finals, which pitted her against the power hitting of the up-and-coming American star Lindsay Davenport. It took all of Seles's concentration to win the match, but in doing so she pulled a groin muscle—one more injury to nurse.

Still, Seles arrived at the Australian Open in Melbourne with reason to be confident. After all, before the stabbing, she had won this tournament three times in a row. Why not four? Except for the badly aching groin muscle, she was in good shape and was sure of herself. Her new attitude showed in her playing, as she reached the semifinals with relative ease. Seles knew that in this run for the championship, she would not have to face her old foe Steffi Graf in the finals. Plagued by injuries, Graf had withdrawn from the Australian Open for the second year in a row, having had foot surgery the month before.

But even if she wanted to, Seles had little time to be sympathetic about Graf's problems. She had new health problems of her own. During a practice for her upcoming semifinal match with American Chanda Rubin, a 19-year-old with an explosive game, Seles found she had difficulty moving her left arm. It was tendonitis again, this time located in her shoulder.

Not sure she could even serve, Seles faced Chanda Rubin the next day. The younger player took the first set. Seles could see the match getting away from her. Willing the pain in her shoulder to go away, she rallied to win the second set and bring the match to a tie. By taking 15 of the last 18 points in the third set, Seles advanced to the finals.

This time she faced another old foe, the hard-hitting Anke Huber. Although Huber broke Seles's serve almost immediately to lead the first set, Seles did not allow the

German player to deny her comeback victory. Monica took the Australian Open for the fourth time, winning the next two sets, 6–4, 6–1. It was her ninth Grand Slam victory, yet Seles couldn't help feeling surprised at her achievement. She commented afterward, "I cannot believe, still, that I'm here."

Monica Seles was indeed back. But what started out as a promising year on the way to number one and a sweep of the Grand Slams was about to hit some snags.

After the Australian Open, Monica decided to travel to Tokyo, Japan, to take part in another tournament. Many fans later questioned why she participated in the event. The French Open, the second of the Grand Slams, was less than four months away. With her nagging injuries, rest might have been a better choice. But Seles opted for Tokyo, and during the tournament she re-injured her shoulder. As a result, she did not enter tournament play again until just one week before the 1996 French Open.

The Monica Seles who walked onto the red clay of Stade Roland Garros outside of Paris did not play well enough to protect her 25-game winning streak, which came to an end at the French Open against Jana Novotna, 7–6, 6–3.

With Seles gone, the field was open to Steffi Graf, who fought a memorable championship with Arantxa Sanchez-Vicario, the two-fisted powerhouse from Spain. The match lasted three hours and four minutes, a French Open women's record. In one of the truly memorable finals, Graf pulled it out, 6–3, 6–7, 10–8.

There was little time for Monica to lament over the loss in Paris with Wimbledon following in June. This was Seles's first appearance there since 1992, and she eagerly looked forward to her return. But Wimbledon, too, proved to be a great disappointment. In the second round, Monica met Katarina Studenikova of Slovakia, rated number 59 in the world. Seles was sent home after a 7–5, 5–7, 6–4 battle. This was the earliest exit for Seles from a major tournament since 1990, when she had lost in the third round at the U.S. Open.

With two bodyguards close behind, Monica leaves the court after losing a quarter-final game in the 1996 French Open. Security became much tighter at tournaments after Monica was stabbed in 1993.

Still, Monica was aware that the year could still be salvaged if she won the U.S. Open. There she made the finals, where once again she faced Steffi Graf. A trimmer, stronger Graf kept Seles running on the court, and Graf took the title, 7–5, 6–4.

The year continued to take its toll. That November, in Oakland, California, Monica was beaten by Martina Hingis, a Czechoslovakian-born phenomenon who had been named for Navratilova. An up-and-coming star, Hingis would attain the number four rank by the year's end, having become at 15 years old the youngest ever doubles champion at Wimbledon (won with Helena Sukova). When Hingis beat Seles in Oakland, 6–2, 6–0, it was especially devastating. For the first time since November 1990, Seles suffered a love set (a set in which the loser doesn't win any games). It was only the fourth "love loss" of her entire career.

Monica's professional tennis year ended in mid-November with the Chase Championships, played indoors at Madison Square Garden in New York City, where her sore shoulder caused her to withdraw from the games. She did, however, agree to play in an exhibition match in December. That decision proved disastrous when she broke the finger on her right hand during the contest.

The year 1996 had been rocky at best. She had not regained her number one ranking; at year's end she shared the number two rank with Sanchez-Vicario, behind Steffi Graf. She was nursing aggravating injuries again, and she was not in great playing shape. But the important thing was that she was back. She had survived a frightful stabbing and a long depression. She was 23 years old and one step away from getting right back on top of the tennis world.

Fervent fans clamor for an autograph as Monica waves to other spectators at the 1998 French Open.

8

STILL GOING FOR
THE GRAND SLAM

IN HER AUTOBIOGRAPHY, Monica Seles observes, "Being number one has never been a goal for me. My goal has always been to do well at Grand Slams. A rank is just a number on a piece of paper, but when you win a Grand Slam, there is so much excitement and emotion . . . holding up a trophy before a stadium of cheering fans, now that's thrilling."

Today, the dream—realistic or otherwise—of every tennis player is still to win the Grand Slam—taking the Australian, French, Wimbledon, and U.S. Open championships all in one year. It is clearly a remarkable accomplishment, as only three women (Maureen Connolly, Margaret Smith Court, and Steffi Graf) and two men (Don Budge and Rod Laver) have ever done it in the singles ranks.

John "Don" Budge is on nearly everyone's list of the all-time tennis greats. Born in Oakland, California, in 1915, he was more interested in baseball and football than in tennis while growing up. But when he discovered the game, he quickly rose to the top ranks.

By 1937, he was ranked number one amateur in the country. He turned down offers to go professional in 1938, which would be his best year. Beginning with the Australian Open, which he won against John Bromwich, 6–4, 6–2, 6–1, he defeated Roderich Menzel of Czechoslovakia at the French Open, 6–3, 6–2, 6–4, and then went to Wimbledon, where he did not lose a single set. His foe was Bunny Austin of Great Britain, who went down, 6–1, 6–0, 6–3. Budge headed home for the U.S. Open and a chance at the Grand Slam. This time he gave up one set to Gene Mako, but won the match—and the Grand Slam—6–3, 6–8, 6–2, 6–1. He was the first tennis player to do so.

The second Grand Slam champion was the darling of the U.S. tennis courts, Maureen Connolly, known as Little Mo. Some say she was the best female player ever. Born in San Diego, California, in 1934, she grew up to be a rather small five feet, four inches. But her ground strokes were surprisingly devastating, and they earned her the nickname Little Mo, referring to the mighty battleship USS *Missouri*, which saw extensive action during World War II. At 16 years, 11 months old, Connolly became the youngest U.S. Open champ ever, a distinction she held until 1979 when Tracy Austin won the event at 16 years, 9 months. Seles would later overtake Austin. In her Grand Slam year, 1953, Little Mo lost only one set in all four tournaments. She beat Julie Sampson, 6–3, 6–2, at the Australian Open. After that tournament she faced and defeated Doris Hart at the French Open, 6–2, 6–4; Wimbledon, 8–6, 7–5; and U.S. Open, 6–2, 6–4. In 1954, a traffic accident ended her career, and she later died of cancer at the age of 34.

Australian Rod Laver won the Grand Slam twice, the only player ever to do so. Born in Queensland in 1938, he was a scrawny, sickly child who grew to a height of just five feet, eight inches, but he certainly could pound the tennis ball. In his 1962 Grand Slam, he played as an

Margaret Smith Court is one of five tennis players in history who have won all four Grand Slam titles in a single year. Here, the Australian receives a trophy after winning the U.S. Open in 1969.

amateur, turning pro the next year. In 1969, his finest year ever, he beat Andres Gimeno for the Australian Open title, Ken Rosewall for the French Open, John Newcombe at Wimbledon, and Tony Roche in a U.S. Open match where the weather was so murky and the court so bad that Laver wore spikes.

A year after Laver, another Australian, Margaret Smith Court, became the fourth Grand Slam champion and second female winner. Born in New South Wales in 1942, she grew to nearly six feet tall and demonstrated astounding strength and coordination. Court set a blazing pace during her Grand Slam year, winning 21 of 27 tournaments. In 1970, she beat Kerry Melville Reid at the Australian Open, Helga Niessen at the French Open, Billie Jean King at Wimbledon, and Rosemary Casals at the U.S. Open. At Wimbledon, Court and King battled through one of the finest women's matches ever, 14–12, 11–9. It was certainly the longest match, and through it all Court played on a severely sprained ankle.

The last of the Grand Slam champs is German-born Steffi Graf, who took the four titles in 1988. Born in Neckarau, in 1969, before her retirement in 1998 she was the fastest of all female players and one of the game's all-time greats. In her Grand Slam year, she beat Chris Evert, 6–1,7–6, in the Australian Open; Natalia Zveveva in the French, 6–0, 6–0; Martina Navratilova at Wimbledon, 5–7, 6–2, 6–1; and Gabriela Sabatini, 6–3, 3–6, 6–1, at the U.S. Open.

These five people hold the highest achievement in the sport of tennis. Could Monica Seles become number six? She has the ability, but other factors such as injuries and strong competition from rising new stars would affect the outcome.

When Seles withdrew from the Chase Championships late in 1996, she considered shoulder surgery. But that would have meant taking several months off from the tour, and Seles was not about to risk that when she had just returned.

With high hopes, she looked forward to an injury-free 1997. She skipped the Australian Open, partly to recover fully from a broken finger and other injuries and partly to spend as much time as possible with her father, whose stomach cancer had begun to spread in 1996. Seles spent as much time as she could by his side, but continued to play tournaments because she knew her continued participation in the pro tour would make him happy. At the same time, she would feel guilty for being away. His death in Sarasota, Florida, on May 14, 1998, was a great setback on her own road to recovery.

In 1997, Seles entered the French Open, where she lost to Hingis in the third round, and she competed at Wimbledon, where she also lost in the third round. It began to look as though the comeback, short-lived as it was, was over. But that August, she took her first title at a tournament in Los Angeles. The next week she took the doubles trophy (with partner Ai Sugiyama) in Tokyo—the fifth doubles title of her career. She was the runner-up at tournaments held in Madrid, Spain, and San Diego, California, and by year's end had qualified once again for the Chase Championships. However, she lost at Madison Square Garden to Arantxa Sanchez-Vicario and fell to number five in the rankings.

At the French Open in 1998, a leaner, fitter Monica Seles, seemingly more dedicated since the death of her father, upset Martina Hingis in the semifinals. However, in the finals she lost once again to Sanchez-Vicario.

Although she kept busy playing in tournament after tournament in 1998, Seles regained some of the weight she had lost after her father's death. The extra pounds may have slowed her down again, and she reached only the quarterfinals at both Wimbledon and the U.S. Open. Back and shoulder problems plagued her once again, but at the Chase Championships, although she lost, she played a thrilling quarterfinals match against Steffi Graf and was voted WTA Comeback Player of the Year for a second time. Nonetheless, the year had been a difficult one, with the sad loss of her father and some tennis setbacks as well.

Monica's fans rallied in her support, as evidenced by a story in a September 1998 issue of *Sports Illustrated.* It observed how Seles had dealt bravely with the loss of part of her career and of a close father who also was her longtime coach, and how because she succeeded in

After the long recovery from the 1993 stabbing, Monica took another blow when her father died of cancer in 1998.

surmounting these difficulties, she has become a celebrity whom everyone can relate to: "Monica has found herself engulfed by a tide of public affection that's touching and extreme. Every week brings more mail from people telling how they, too, have lost a parent, a sister, a child. No one is shy. Every trip to the store brings a story about how much someone admires her." *Sports Illustrated* called Monica Seles "one of the most beloved women in her sport."

Monica began 1999 at the Australian Open, seeded number six. After beating Graf in the quarterfinals, she lost to Hingis, 6–2, 6–4, in the semifinals. In May, at the Bausch & Lomb Championships in Amelia Island, Florida, she beat Ruxandra Dragomir in the finals, 6–2, 6–3. She drew a fourth seed for the French Open that year, but was bounced out in the semifinals by Graf in three sets. Seles did not get nearly that far at Wimbledon, where she was seeded number four and lost to Mirjana Lucic, 7–6, 7–6.

But Monica hoped to improve her ranking in 1999 by taking the U.S. Open that September. Seeded fourth, she faced Jennifer Capriati. A powerful tennis player in her teens, Capriati had suffered serious problems with drug and alcohol addiction that forced her to take a very early retirement from tennis. At the U.S. Open she was attempting a comeback, while her opponent Monica Seles was trying to put aside her own emotional and physical burdens. The round 16 match would turn out to be the most emotional of the tournament, with the winner advancing to the semifinals. For a while, time seemed to stand still on the hard courts. The air was full of flying tennis balls, grunts and sighs, and the cheers of fans. In the end, Seles won the match fairly easily, 6–4, 6–3, and made her way to the quarterfinals.

After the Capriati match, Seles talked to reporters. She said she was glad that Capriati, like herself, was back in tennis after an extended absence. "I got stabbed when I was No. 1 in the world, winning all the tournaments," Seles said. "No other player in history had to deal with that. I don't like to go back there. But right now I'm just happy where I am and playing good tennis. What's past is past. Jennifer had a layoff for a different reason. Things happen in your life. . . . We're just here and trying to change the future."

At the quarterfinals, Monica met the younger sister of two rising tennis stars, 19-year-old Venus Williams and 17-year-old Serena Williams. Somewhat unexpectedly, seventh-seeded Serena had advanced over her older sister Venus into the quarterfinals. For some time, the tennis world had been watching these two promising, extremely talented players from California. Venus had made her tennis debut in 1994 at the age of 14, and she showed great promise on the tennis courts. However, her father, who like Monica's father coached his children, hinted that of the two, the younger Serena was really the more talented, perhaps more dedicated player.

That prediction seemed to come true when Serena faced Seles. At the start it seemed as though first-time jitters and youthful excitement would get the better of the teenager. She lost the first set, and Seles fans began to think that Monica would take this one. But Serena settled down and began to show the steady strength that would become her trademark. With an impressive show of muscles and consistency, she got the better of a tiring Seles, achieving a 4–6, 6–3, 6–2 victory.

After her loss to Williams at the U.S. Open, Seles admitted to feeling somewhat "older" on the court. She said of Williams, "She's a lot stronger than I am and gets the ball back a lot better." Her statement is a sign of the athlete who has nursed the injuries and pain for a long time but repeatedly tries to get that edge just once more. At the beginning of her career, with the possible exception of Steffi Graf, Seles really had no equal on the court. She had relentless returns, strength and sureness in her strokes, and confidence in their placement. Today, she must rely even more on intelligence, experience, and grit. It's not easy. In her mid-20s, which for the sport is old, the climb back to the top is a steep path.

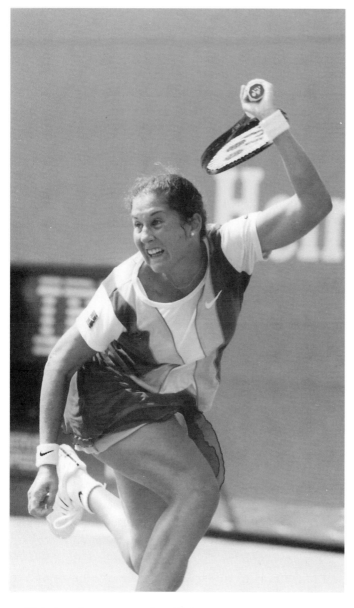

Monica chases down a tough baseline shot. In her mid-20s, Monica today faces ever-greater challenges against the younger, up-and-coming stars of women's tennis.

If Seles does return, it will be a tough journey during which she may have to put aside her other interests. She's not only a competitor on the courts, but a shrewd businesswoman off the courts as well.

Following up on her interest in designer clothes,

Monica has begun creating some of her own styles. She also has signed contracts to endorse various products, including Perrier mineral water, Nike sneakers, and No ExCuses jeans. When her father was still living, she had re-signed a contract with Fila, making sure that the company chose her father to design the sports logo. She was the first athlete to serve as spokesperson for Matrix Essentials, a line of beauty products. Clearly, Monica Seles has a lot going for her.

Is it all too much? Just before the 1999 U.S. Open, in its September 9 issue, *Newsday* ran a lengthy article on Monica Seles, focusing on her infamous grunt. The article noted that in the early days of her entry into professional tennis, the grunt had become her trademark. It was something she seemed unable to control, a sound that followed a two-fisted backhand blast or a ripping forehand down the line. Seles's grunt would instill aggravation and sometimes fear in her opponents. But, according to the *Newsday* reporter, the grunt today may just mean she's getting tired. After the stabbing in 1993, the story claimed, something left the champion, something that perhaps would never return.

At issue is not only the stabbing incident or the many injuries that have long plagued Seles, but also her age. The career of a professional sports figure is very short. Seles was not quite 26 years old when she stepped on court for the U.S. Open in 1999; that may be young in some sports careers, but not in professional tennis. There's always somebody younger and stronger waiting in the wings—up-and-coming stars like Martina Hingis, Lindsay Davenport, or Venus and Serena Williams.

Even Seles herself admits that, although her strokes are still there, she just doesn't cover the court quite as completely as she used to do. Can she make up for that? One thing she's always had, the *Newsday* article points out, even when her body has failed her, is her mind. No one was ever tougher on the grass at Wimbledon, the red clay of Paris, or the hard courts of New York City. She played the game at its finest with her own kind of rage, a determination that would not back down, a drive that would not give in until the last ball was chased down and the last point was decided.

That's the Monica Seles her fans know. That's the Monica Seles they come to see. That's the Monica Seles who is a champion.

CHRONOLOGY

1973   Monica Seles is born in Novi Sad, Yugoslavia, on December 2, to Karolj and Esther Seles

1983   Wins Yugoslav 12-and-under championship at age 9

1984   Wins European 12-and-under championship at age 10

1985   Becomes first athlete under 18 years old to be named Yugoslavian Sportswoman of the Year at age 11

1986   Moves to United States to attend Nick Bollettieri Tennis Academy in Bradenton, Florida

1988   Plays in first amateur tournament, Virginia Slims, in Boca Raton, Florida

1989   Turns professional at age 15 in February; in April wins first pro tournament at Virginia Slims tournament in Houston, Texas, beating number one seed Chris Evert

1990   Becomes youngest woman to win French Open, youngest player to win Grand Slam event in more than 100 years; named Corel WTA Tour Most Improved Player

1991   Wins three of four Grand Slam events—the Australian, French, and U.S. Opens; becomes youngest woman to win Australian Open and youngest player to receive number one world ranking; becomes second youngest player to win U.S. Open; named 1991 Associated Press Female Athlete of the Year

1992   Repeats as champion at the Australian, French, and U.S. Opens

1993   Wins at Australian Open; on April 30 is stabbed at Citizen Cup tournament in Hamburg, Germany; retires from tennis

1994   Becomes U.S. citizen on March 16

1995   Returns to Corel WTA Tour competition co-ranked with Steffi Graf as number one, wins the Canadian Open in August; reaches finals of U.S. Open; named one of *People* magazine's Most Intriguing People of 1995; voted Professional Female Athlete of the year by fans; named *Tennis Magazine* Comeback Player of the Year and Corel WTA TOUR Comeback Player of the Year

1996   Wins fourth Australian Open but develops tendonitis in shoulder, competes in first Olympic Games; sustains the worst results of her career at Wimbledon, where she loses in second round; releases book *Monica: From Fear to Victory* in June

1997 Does not compete in Australian Open due to broken finger

1998 Earns 400th career match victory; becomes fourth woman to earn more than $10 million in prize money; wins fourth consecutive Canadian Open title; reaches quarterfinals at Wimbledon; reaches the finals at the French Open, just three weeks after her father's death; elected to WTA Tour Players' Council for 1998–99

1999 Reaches semifinals of Australian Open; is semifinalist at French Open

2000 Wins bronze medal in Olympic Games in Sydney, Australia, by defeating Jelena Dokie

2001 Reaches quarterfinals of Australian Open, where she loses to eventual Open winner Jennifer Capriati

CAREER STATISTICS

Major titles:

1990   French singles

1991   Australian singles
French singles
U.S. singles

1992   Australian singles
French singles
U.S. singles

1993   Australian singles

1996   Australian singles

Career highlights:

1989   Reaches French Open semifinals

1990   Youngest champion of French Open and WTA Most Improved Player award

1991   Australian, French, U.S. titles; youngest to take Australian; ranked number one; Player of the Year

1992   Australian, French, U.S. titles and Player of the Year

1995   Wins Comeback Player of the Year and Most Exciting Player

1996   Australian Open title

1997   Reaches French Open finals and Comeback Player of the Year

1999   Reaches Australian Open semifinals; reaches Pan Pacific semifinals; wins Amelia Island title; reaches French Open semifinals; reaches Du Maurier Open finals; reaches U.S. Open quarterfinals

2000   Wins bronze medal at Olympic Games, Sydney, Australia

2001   Reaches Australian Open quarterfinals

FURTHER READING

Books

Aronson, Virginia. *Venus and Serena Williams.* Philadelphia: Chelsea House, 2000.

Collins, Bud, and Zander Hollander. *Bud Collins' Tennis.* Detroit, Mich.: Visible Ink, 1997.

Douglas, Paul. *Learn Tennis in a Weekend.* New York: Knopf, 1992.

Martin, Marvin: *Arthur Ashe: Of Tennis and the Human Spirit.* New York: Impact, 1999.

Murdico, Suzanne J. *Monica Seles.* Austin, Texas: Raintree, 1998.

Rutledge, Rachel. *Women of Sports: The Best of the Best in Tennis.* Brookfield, Conn.: Millbrook, 1998.

Seles, Monica, and Nancy Ann Richardson. *Monica: From Fear to Victory.* New York: HarperCollins, 1996.

Teitelbaum, Michael. *Grand Slam Stars: Martina Hingis and Venus Williams.* New York: Harper, 1996.

Truman, Christine. *Tennis.* Morristown, N.J.: Silver-Burdett, 1987.

Websites

Monica Seles
http://monica-seles.com/

Women's Tennis Association
http://www.wtatour.com

APPENDIX

FINDING OUT MORE ABOUT POST-TRAUMATIC STRESS DISORDER

Books:

Allen, Jon G. *Coping with Trauma: A Guide to Self-Understanding.* New York: American Psychiatric Press, 1999.

Flannery, Raymond. *Post-Traumatic Stress Disorder: The Victim's Guide to Healing and Recovery.* New York: Crossroad Publishing Company, 1996..

Fullerton, C.S. and Ursano, R. J. *Post–traumatic Stress Disorder: Acute and Long-Term Responses to Trauma and Disaster.* Washington, D.C.: American Psychiatric Press, 1997.

Herman, J. L. *Trauma and Recovery.* New York: Basic Books, 1992.

Matsakis, Aphrodite. *I Can't Get Over It: A Handbook for Trauma Survivors.* New York: New Harbinger Publications, 1992.

———. *Trust After Trauma: A Guide to Relationships for Survivors and Those Who Love Them.* New York: Harbinger Publications, 1998.

Parkinson, Frank. *Post-Trauma Stress: Recovery from Hidden Emotional Damage Caused by Violence and Disaster.* Cambridge, Mass.: Fisher Books, 2000.

Websites:

National Center for Post-Traumatic Stress Disorder
http://www.ncptsd.org

National Institute of Mental Health: Post-Traumatic Stress Disorder
http://www.nimh.nih.gov/anxiety/anxiety/ptsd/

INDEX

Rose Blue is the author of numerous books for children and young adults. Two of her books were adapted for young people's specials aired on NBC television. She is a graduate of Brooklyn College with a master's degree from Bank Street College of Education.

Corinne J. Naden, a graduate of New York University, is a freelance writer and editor. A former journalist in the U.S. Navy and children's book editor in New York City, she has written and co-authored more than 60 books for children and young adults.

James Scott Brady serves on the board of trustees with the Center to Prevent Handgun Violence and is the vice chairman of the Brain Injury Foundation. Mr. Brady served as assistant to the President and White House press secretary under President Ronald Reagan. He was severely injured in an assassination attempt on the president, but remained the White House press secretary until the end of the administration. Since leaving the White House, Mr. Brady has lobbied for stronger gun laws. In November 1993, President Bill Clinton signed the Brady Bill, a national law requiring a waiting period on handgun purchases and a background check on buyers.

PICTURE CREDITS